The War on Normal

How to Find Contentment
in Your Post-Baby Body

JENNY BAKER & SARAH BLIGHT

JENNY BAKER & SARAH BLIGHT

We dedicate this book to all the loads of laundry, the myriad of meals prepared, booboos we kissed, tantrums we diffused, endless errands we ran and all of the nights we didn't write because of pure exhaustion. If it weren't for all of you, this book would have been finished 2 years ago.

JB & SB

JENNY BAKER & SARAH BLIGHT

Table of Contents

JENNY BAKER & SARAH BLIGHT

It's All About Freedom

Our stories are different. Our struggles are not the same. But there is a common thread: freedom. We just want freedom from the "normal" post-baby thoughts and feelings. We grow tired opening magazines and seeing headlines boasting of celebrities finding their pre-baby weight just weeks after delivery or running marathons without soaking their pants in pee. We feel taken captive by this unspoken "normal" standard to which we're subconsciously submitting. And because of this, one cold January night through a series of long and inspired text messages, Jenny and I decided to run headlong into this struggle together and invite other moms to join us.

In writing this book, we discovered answers might not be as important as we'd once believed; and the whole *"it's the journey, not the destination"* saying came to life and rang true in new ways (no matter how cliché and cheesy it sounds.) We decided to forgo solutions and start with questions. While writing, we peeled away our layers and examined what lies at the heart of us, the heart of our self-doubt, self-neglect, self-love, self-worth and the way we see ourselves. We found that the process of question asking and digging deep is where the perspective, healing, and growth came from, despite the long, painful, and joyful road.

We've learned that the most helpful thing we can offer you is our partnership: two moms in the same boat. We commit to being vulnerable while sharing the tools we've found helpful in navigating this jungle of post-baby body image—recognizing we're not experts—merely partners in the trenches.

We both have battle scars to share and victory stories that shape us and guide how we think, feel, and act. As Sarah likes to say, get ready mamas, because we're getting ready to show you what's under our proverbial kimonos.

Let's be honest: writing this book has been hard. It's uncovered our secret insecurities, fear, and shame. It's forced us to get honest with ourselves, each other, our partners, and even our kids. It's also renewed our belief in the importance and power of vulnerability among women. Our struggle is noble and big and can have an impact on hundreds of women who will come after us. Most importantly, it can have an impact on our hearts, in our homes, and in our relationships.

Even though it's been uncomfortable, we're all in because we want this book to be different, to make a difference. I (Jenny) struggle with most traditional self-help books. Often their well-intentioned 3, 5, 7 or 10-step programs give me a list of things to do without ever addressing the underlying reasons I've gotten myself to a place of needing the steps in the first place. Some of them are simply behavior modification programs.

As you'll hear later in our stories, we've found that managing behavior never gets to the core of the matter. Managing behavior is like cutting off the fruit of a tree and expecting the tree to die. Trees only die when completely uprooted. That's why most dieting plans don't work. They give us actions to perform without helping us process our feelings, the ones that trigger the unhealthy behaviors and choices.

To find contentment in our bodies, a total uprooting is necessary. This means our book won't just be practical steps towards modifying our behavior, but will also be a journey of recognizing our unhelpful beliefs about our bodies and then digging those up and getting rid of them. We'll do this through storytelling, research sharing, and focused journal activities—all of which will guide our thoughts, feelings and actions towards meaningful personal growth.

Our biggest goal for this journey is deeper contentment with our post-baby bodies. We'll get there by:

1. Connecting, with other moms who are in this fight.
2. Being inspired and challenged towards life change.
3. Discovering tangible tools to grow and make those changes.

If there's a freedom scale with 1 being trapped by constant discontentment, and 10 being total contentment—our hope is after walking down this road together—we've all at least moved closer towards 10. If you're a 2 now, we hope you'll be a 3 by the time you read the last page. Movement is how we measure growth and success.

At times this process could feel scary and invasive. **Ya'll, it's going to get uncomfortable before it gets**

meaningful. Grab a friend or 2 and do this together. This book and really this journey are meant to be shared.

Please mama—we beg of you—don't go down this road alone. Walk with us and your friends, your people, your tribe. If you don't know who those people might be, take a deep breath, summon some bravery, and step out and invite 1 or 2 ladies you think would be down with this journey, to read this book with you.

Thanks for joining us in finding contentment with our post-baby bodies. Let's hit it!

Sarah and Jenny

1

The Myth of Normal

Normal is an illusion.
What is normal for the spider is chaos for the fly.

CHARLES ADDAMS

It was a cold and tense November morning in
Manhattan, NY. The Continental Army, led by General
George Washington, was in trouble, and all American
fighters had been called to help. The mood that morning
was intense, and all men, including John Corbin, were on
high alert.

Corbin was a Virginia farmer, and had joined the army
the previous year when the Revolutionary War began. He
used his farming skills to become specialized in loading
and firing guns. But John didn't just bring his rock star
farming skills with him, he also brought a secret weapon:
his wife, Margaret. Margaret would not be left behind
and was adamant that she fight alongside her hubby.

The fight for freedom wasn't just important to John, but also to Margaret, and she was willing to use everything she had to help. She was a freedom fighter.

So, while John trained, Margaret cared for the soldiers by feeding, clothing, and even medically treating them. By all accounts, this woman was incredibly strong both physically and emotionally, and even ended up helping with battlefield strategy sessions. You go, Margaret!

One Saturday, November 16th to be exact, everything changed for Margaret and for the American Army.

That morning the British started attacking like crazy, coming from all sides. John Corbin started manning the cannons, loading and firing with the help of his partner, until Corbin's partner was killed. It was then that Margaret stepped onto the field, next to her husband, and together they fought. Talk about brave. She believed in the pursuit of freedom, and it meant more to her than her comfort or even life.

With courage and extreme fearlessness, John would fire the cannon and Margaret would load it. Sadly, it wasn't long before John was shot and killed, leaving Margaret with no time to grieve. Thinking quickly, she began manning the cannon herself—both loading and firing at the opposition. Her aim was so accurate that she drew the attention of British soldiers, who began targeting her. Yet even that wouldn't stop her! She kept firing even when defeat was imminent. Eventually, Margaret was severely wounded, her left arm becoming useless. But a left arm was a small price to pay for freedom.

Margaret survived to see the war end and America claim its freedom from British rule. She was recognized as the first woman to take a soldier's place in the war for liberty and the first woman to fight in the Revolutionary War. Freedom was something she stood for and willingly walked onto the battlefield to claim.

While she was ridiculously brave, Margaret wasn't the first woman to fight against oppression, and she certainly isn't the last. In fact, whether we see it or not, as moms, we're in a battle. It looks, feels, and is fought differently, but the resounding goal is the same: Freedom.

Now, we know a war story is an odd way to start a body after baby book for women. Yet it's the best example we've found to represent what our post-partum body journey often looks and feels like—a war for freedom. We recognize there are different degrees of war happening in the world around us: there are women who are in the midst of political war, there are women who are fighting poverty and hunger, women fighting oppression, there are women who are in the midst of a parenting or custody war, and there are women who are in the midst of a mental war between the choice to eat or starve themselves. All are valid, deep, and incredibly personal.

For us, calling "the post-partum body image fight," a war, validates the depth and seriousness of our journey. We wake up each morning and face the opposition as we turn on the TV, our computers, and read our magazines. We walk onto the battlefield every day as we get dressed

13

and catch a glimpse of ourselves in the mirror. We struggle as our kids ask us questions and listen intently to how we talk, think, and feel about our bodies. Freedom in our homes, in our marriages, in our friendships, and the way we parent begins with the way we view ourselves and the outcome affects how we navigate other battles in our lives.

Who and What are We Fighting?

Mama, we know there's a struggle with our post-baby bodies because we feel and see its effects in our behaviors, in the rampant way eating disorders are emerging in our Western culture, along with dissatisfaction, comparison, and the pressure to be "perfect." These issues beg the question, "Who's behind this? What's working against us?"

We believe the answer to this question is, "normal." "Normal" cultivates discontentment, and discontentment breeds struggle.

Great. But what does "normal" even mean? According to the trusty ole dictionary, "normal" means "*according to a rule,*" and its reach permeates every industry, socio-economic level, and decision-making processes in the Western world. "Normal" has become the measuring stick for the way we view our bodies, our financial status, our kids' health and growth, our academic achievement, and even our career goals.

Jenny and I started asking ourselves, *"But does 'normal' really exist?"* There are statistical majorities. There are researched and proven best practices. There might even be a "typical" or a general trend or set of experiences. However, what all research shows is without a doubt there is no "normal."

Now, there are realities in our lives and in our bodies that make us feel like we have a "normal", or a "normal for me." Those "normals" can be further defined as thoughts and feelings we most consistently experience. Our constants. Our baseline. There are times when acknowledging our unique baseline is helpful to ourselves personally. For example, when we go to the doctor because we know something's off with our health based on what we know about our "normal." But in the context of this book, that's not what we're talking about. What seems to motivate us, while also giving us the ultimate beat down, is comparing our "normal", to someone else's "normal." Comparisons cripple us, and so our fight is against our tendency to hear, absorb, and own other people's baselines.

Shared Experience

Regardless of what our pregnancy and birth journeys have been, we, as women, have experienced something powerful. We've accomplished something so unique to our own body and life, that replicating it isn't even a

JENNY BAKER & SARAH BLIGHT

possibility. "Different" is the only constant from mom to mom. Even if we didn't have our ideal labor and delivery experience, we still walk away changed, with a new perspective. Let's acknowledge for a sec that what we've done is pretty impressive. *High Five*Butt Slap*

As we come off the high of meeting the new life our bodies grew and birthed, (sigh)...those wonderful, juicy, delicious endorphins and hormones that coursed through our bodies start to diminish. We start to heal while simultaneously peeling the layers off our post-partum selves. We're ready to get back into the rhythm of life and return to "normal." It's in this transition that the miracle we've experienced evaporates and becomes incredibly insignificant in comparison to our insecurities and self-doubt. Suddenly none of that matters as we look in the mirror and feel disgust with what we see looking back at us.

And then, the guilt comes in...like a flood. The guilt about our feelings towards how our bodies look and function washes over us in an instant. We feel like we've betrayed ourselves, to ourselves.

The struggle is real and this is what it feels like. In talking to moms all over the place, this is a resounding theme. We've all been here at some point or another and it sucks.

We're led to believe there's a post-partum "normal," a set of rules by which to measure our success. As we internalize this belief, we find ourselves greatly lacking, which feels like failure, which leads us to becoming discontent with how our lives are trending.

Using someone else's constant to define our success is harmful and most definitely doesn't lead to positive thoughts and feelings, but to hurt and pain. And while that doesn't sound so ominous and scary, the tentacles of discontentment can reach into crevices and places that may not be so apparent to us. The effects are far reaching and frankly, devastating.

We talked to one mom named Alison, who has two kids age 9 months and 2 ½ years. She said this about her body just a few months after giving birth:

> *"[I was] Disappointed. Once again, I put the expectation on myself that I would be one of those people who has the weight just melt off because I was breastfeeding. Not so much. I thought I would be back in my normal sizes and never was. Everything is squishy-er, everywhere. Even though I've lost some weight, it doesn't come off in the right places."*

I (Sarah) was chatting with the founder of the 4th Trimester Body project, Ashlee Wells Jackson, recently and she explained that when our outcome doesn't match up with our expectation, then suddenly it becomes "not normal" to us.

As American cartoonist, Charles Addams (creator of the Addams family) wrote in the quote at the beginning of this chapter, *"Normal is an illusion. What is normal for the spider is chaos for the fly."* This is solid advice to remember

17

as we navigate the meaning of normal and how it impacts us.

The Three Ds

If "normal" doesn't exist but we're all trying to embrace our new post-partum "normal", then that creates an obvious tension with the title of this book, *The War on Normal*. (See why it took us 2 years to write this thing?)

So let's talk Santa for a moment. As kids, if we believed in Santa, we lived and died for Christmas morning. Our parents would even leverage Santa's existence to manipulate us into good manners and obedience throughout the year. We modified our behavior based on our belief that Santa existed.

Then we grew up and we have "normal," which in this analogy, is the adult Santa. "Normal" isn't real but we seem to modify our behavior based on its existence. We all believed "normal" existed and now, Sarah and I are the kids on your street about to burst your bubble and tell you it's all a lie.

Pursuing someone else's definition of "normal" creates our struggle and leads us to experience what we call the 3 D's: deception, distraction, and disconnection.

Deception

As parents, we spend tons and tons of energy making sure our kids follow through with what we've asked of them. When we see our kids acting out behaviors that aren't in line with our belief systems, we focus our discipline efforts to alter those behaviors.

It's very much the same with us adults. When we believe something is insufficient, we attempt to rectify it through action. While certain change is good and healthy, there's plenty that isn't. Change **can be** motivated by untruth. In our research, we found that there's ample evidence showing that many of us moms believe the lies that our post-partum bodies are inadequate, insufficient, and lacking.

Let's take a look at patterns of cultural change starting with the big picture. According to The American Society for Aesthetic Plastic Surgery[i]:

- Since 1997, there has been a 274% increase in the total number of cosmetic procedures.
- In 2014 women had more than 9.6 million cosmetic procedures.
- The number of non-surgical procedures for women increased over 429% from 1997.
- The top 5 surgical procedures for women were: Liposuction, Breast Augmentation, Tummy Tuck, Eyelid Surgery and Breast Lift.

Americans have spent more than 12 billion dollars during each calendar year in 2013 and 2014 on combined surgical and nonsurgical procedures.

*Here's the deal with these statistics. We're not saying plastic surgery is bad. We're not saying women who undergo cosmetic procedures are bad. Looking at these statistics, we do believe discontentment is a major motivator that most often leads to people seeking cosmetic procedures in order to change an outward appearance.

According to an article in the *Huffington Post*[ii], researchers at the University of North Carolina found only 12.2% of women over 50 are happy with how their body looks.

Looking at these stats, it seems that feeling discontentment with our bodies and choosing elective cosmetic surgery are common. Talk about deception. These stats speak very loudly to the lie we buy into when we believe our bodies aren't enough.

As we researched this topic, we were wondering if we were the only moms (other than those in these stats) who were feeling deceived. We weren't sure to what extent our friends could relate. This curiosity prompted us to ask our friends and other moms what their post-partum body experience has been like in the form of a survey. Shockingly, hundreds of moms responded and the responses were telling.

When we asked women how they felt about their bodies **before pregnancy**:

- 16% responded in a negative way, suggesting that they did not feel good about their bodies, saying things like *"hated it,"* *"unhappy,"* and *"ashamed."*

- 56% of the ladies responded with language that suggested they felt good about their bodies, using words like *"decent,"* *"not amazing but not negative."*

- 25% used language suggesting that they felt pretty great about their bodies, using words like *"sexy,"* *"confident,"* *"toned,"* *"healthy,"* and *"badass."*

We also asked them how they felt about their bodies **after giving birth**:

- 50% of the women we surveyed used language to convey that they were not at all down with how their body looked, using words like *"gross,"* *"defeated,"* *"weak,"* *"flabbergasted,"* *"awkward,"* *"shocked,"* and *"betrayed."*

- 40% of the women used words like *"mostly okay,"* *"mediocre,"* *"pleasantly surprised,"* and *"fine"* to express how they felt about their bodies post baby.

- Only 8% described their feelings toward their bodies very positively after giving birth, using words like *"way awesome," "loved my body," "higher self-confidence," "perfectly fine,"* and *"happy."*

Friends, we have a serious problem that no one is talking about. Based on statistics alone, us moms are fighting against "normal" and losing terribly to the lie of discontentment. It's mind blowing that we allow "normal" to keep us captive so powerfully!

Yet hidden amongst the lies are truths to be reclaimed. When we asked women what their favorite thing about their post-partum body was, this is what we read:

- *"That I created a life. I grew and nurtured my baby boy with just my body!"* Stacey, mom of 2

- *"I think the fact that I grew these two little people in there, and that my boobs gave them nourishment and comfort. A woman's body is amazing."* Jen, mom of 2.

- *"Mentally just knowing this body carried life! I carried and gave birth to our beautiful daughter!!! There is no greater accomplishment."* Danielle, mom of 1.

The truth is our bodies are amazing. They're strong and capable, beautiful and resilient. Let's not be deceived into believing the lie that they're not. Our contentment requires us to choose to believe the truth, even when it doesn't feel good.

Distraction

I (Sarah) remember sitting cross-legged alongside my mom, "helping" her weed her garden. She taught me what those invasive, pesky weeds looked like. Then she would scold me when I would find them but just pick off the leaves. In my 4-year-old mind, the leaves of the weeds were the eyesores. But to my mama's trained eye, it was what we couldn't see that needed to be uprooted, only then would the weed stop growing and stop strangling out the rest of the healthy, producing plants in the garden.

Our discontentment often times gets manifested in an outlet that has nothing to do with our true struggle. We get distracted. We might be discontent with the way we look in the mirror, and rather than fighting that battle, we decide we need to clean the mirror and commit to a tidier house. Or we buckle down at work and strive to produce at a higher level than before. We could buy new and trendy clothes or new skincare and makeup. Regardless of how we decide to indulge those feelings, we're often distracted from dealing with the true root of our discontentment and instead choose surface fixes. (After all, picking off the leaves is a lot less uncomfortable than digging up the roots.) This distraction also ties into being deceived. We get fooled into believing our post-baby bodies aren't enough and we avoid doing the hard work of uprooting and overcoming the discontentment. Distracting and numbing our pain with quick fixes allow us to move on until the next time we feel pangs of discontentment.

We can't perform better at work, drive a sleeker car, get a bigger house or even get super buff at the gym and expect our feelings of discontentment to go away. It will merely manifest itself in other ways.

Freedom requires us to be avid and effective weed pullers. We need to identify it, grasp our discontentment by the roots, and throw it in the trash. Anyone who has gardened knows that this has to be done over and over and over. Those pesky suckers don't disappear easily. But it's worth the hard work to uproot the lies and plant something new in its place.

Disconnection

Then the kicker comes. Our measuring stick of "normal" convinces us we're so far from successful that no one could ever relate to our struggle. From this lie we isolate and begin living disconnected from safe, healthy, and positive community. The enemy cuts us off from anyone who can speak truth into our lives and we begin to sink deeper into our inner thoughts and emotional captivity. When we do hang out with other moms, we fear authenticity and vulnerability, instead exchanging them for surface smiles and hollow banter. We keep our painful places quiet and believe no one can relate or help (or wants to, for that matter.) "Normal" wins, searing our hearts with deeper discontentment than we've ever felt.

Other moms helped us realize just how **not alone** we really are. Every mom struggles in some form with her post-baby body and to believe anything different is to believe a lie. Here are some of the comments we collected when we asked moms about how they feel about their post-partum bodies:

> *"Disappointing! I'm disappointed in myself for not working harder to get the weight off. And now I've got 30 pounds to lose. I know that may not seem like a lot to some people but it's a lot to me. I've never struggled with having to lose weight and now I feel pretty stuck with not knowing where to start."* Andrea, mom of 2

> *"Frenemies! I'm grateful for all the working parts and bits, and I'm appreciative of all the things it does day in and day out for my family and myself, but I can't say I don't talk sh*t about it behind its back!"* Charity, mom of 2

> *"Like the Facebook status—It's complicated."* Rachael, mom of 3

We also gathered up and listed the words most often used by mamas to describe their feelings about their bodies:

Embarrassed
Tired
Discouraged
Disgust
Foes
Hate
Love-hate

And two of responses just said "HUMPF" and "Ehhhhhh"...(we feel you, ladies.) If we're honest, we've felt every one of those emotions. No, we feel every one of those emotions daily. Isolation keeps us believing the same lie and holds us captive. We must decide to fling open the jail cell doors and invite others into our journey.

Physics proves light and dark can't co-exist. When light is brought into a dark room the darkness is banished. Sharing our struggles with other people sheds light into the dark places in our hearts and brings freedom. We delve more into how to find our community in Chapter 8.

The Goal

In the end, our goal is to view our bodies more positively and move away from embracing another's "normal" as our own, and instead, find peace in our reality.

As we sought to define our objective, we concluded that "contentment" is the one word that encompasses everything for which we're struggling. It's also a word many philosophers have spoken about.

The Greek philosopher Socrates said, "*He who is not contented with what he has, would not be contented with what he would like to have.*"

Another philosopher, Lao Tzu, said,
"Be content with what you have;
rejoice in the way things are.
When you realize there is nothing lacking,
the whole world belongs to you."

And even the Jewish teacher and apostle Paul said while he was in prison, *"I have learned to be content whatever the circumstances. I know what it is to be in need, and I know what it is to have plenty. I have learned the secret of being content in any and every situation, whether well fed or hungry, whether living in plenty or in want."* [iii]

Modern day momosophers, Sarah and Jenny (that's us!), define contentment as:

To be at peace with ourselves. To view our bodies as friends and allies, so that we can work together to accomplish our goal.

We want to grow and replace the discontentment we feel with the freedom contentment brings. For our purposes, we want to measure growth by movement rather than a specific destination. As we mentioned in the intro, we'll be using a 1-10 contentment scale.

How wonderful would it be to look at our post-baby bodies on good days, bloated days, or while looking at our naked bodies in the mirror in front of our kids, and feel contentment no matter what we saw? We believe that as humans, women, and mothers, we deeply desire contentment. We also believe it's within our grasp.

Standing Guard

For 2 years, as we've been digging into this whole topic of contentment with our bodies, we've learned that finding it won't make our lives perfect. It won't erase all our issues; it won't put money in the bank, or give us amazing health, or fix that dysfunctional relationship, or give us glowing skin, or remove that stomach pooch.

But a life of contentment allows us to experience more peace than turmoil. There's no striving in contentment, no running in a hamster wheel, no exasperation at the fruitlessness of chasing a myth. Contentment allows us to bask in the gift of freedom.

Before we go on, we'd like to invite you to pause and spend some time reflecting. At the end of each chapter we'll offer up some questions for you to consider. Our intent here is to help you create a meaningful journey.

Recap

- ✓ The post-partum body image struggle is legit.
- ✓ "Normal" doesn't exist. Just like Santa.
- ✓ When we believe the idea of normal, we experience the 3 Ds: it deceives, distracts, and disconnects us.
- ✓ Freedom is contentment, and this concept is counter-cultural, which is why it's hard and can suck.

✓ Contentment means to be at peace within myself. To view my body as a friend and ally, so that we can work together to accomplish our goal.

Action Steps
Journal or Discuss

When discussing or journaling the following questions, be specific. It's easy to gloss over questions and give vague answers. But the more specific and in-depth you are about your answers, the more helpful it will be to take steps towards growth in that area.

- What does the term "normal" (in a post-baby context) mean to you?

- How does your description line-up with your current post-baby reality?

- How does that make you feel?

- What does contentment look like for you?

- What motivates you toward a life of contentment?

JENNY BAKER & SARAH BLIGHT

2

The Culture Struggle

[It's] hard to feel "good" about looks when our society focuses so harshly on them. Hard to disconnect new body image from self-worth.

ANONYMOUS, mom of 3

In researching and writing, reflecting and sharing, we've found 2 areas where our struggle most powerfully manifests itself: in our culture and our relationships. Our culture is full of values and thought patterns; some we want to adopt and others we choose to reject. Our relationships are also a place we see our struggles come alive as we navigate interpersonal connections amidst our inward battle.

As we move forward, it's important for us to realize that both our culture and our relationships can bring life and be extremely encouraging. They can also get distorted and harm us.

This distinction is important. We can't completely unplug from our society, and living like hermit moms away from people (no matter how much we pray for it) isn't the answer either. Instead of disconnecting, let's attack the destructive patterns that happen within these contexts.

Looking at both of these areas, we'll focus on the harmful patterns of "normal" and how discontentment manifests itself through them. A pattern is something reoccurring, repeated, and regular. This means a pattern of discontentment will show up regularly enough that with some intentionality, we'll be able to identify it and change its impact on our life.

Patterns in our culture, a.k.a. cultural norms, are often passed along through a narrative, or story told to us, repeatedly and over time. There are many stories we hear throughout childhood that are obvious to our conscious and some that aren't. A child who hears the story "*you're always causing trouble*," or "*you're so smart*," begins to believe that message. Those are some of the obvious narratives. There are some sneaky cultural norms that are much harder to identify and fight. We dug up two of these subtle messages in the history of American fashion and what happens in our homes, post-partum.

Sizing Up The Situation

In the 1800s the fashion world orbited around French couture (a fancy word for custom made.) Everything beautiful, elegant, and indulgent came from France, and women swooned over men who would meet them at the docks with lavishly wrapped dress boxes in hand. And can you blame them?

Up until the mid 1800s, American women either sewed their own clothes or went to a couture boutique to have personal dresses made. Clothing sizes didn't exist and models were people who posed for paintings.

And then, in a stroke of genius, retailers like Montgomery Ward, and Sears, Roebuck & Company decided to bring the goods to the ladies and began sending out shopping catalogs to the masses. These guys were makin' bank! However, they quickly realized they were losing tons of cash because women were returning clothes that didn't fit. In an attempt to keep up with demand and minimize returns, they realized they needed some standardization or "normal."

As a remedy, the manufacturing companies asked the Department of Agriculture...yes...the USDA, to standardize clothing sizes. In 1939, a national survey of women's body measurements was conducted and a terribly unscientific and highly discriminatory study ensued. Fifteen thousand women were measured over 59 different places on their bodies. Participants were volunteers who were compensated for their time and because of this, mostly lower-income, white women took part.

The study took 3 years to pull together and in April of 1942, a concise and "helpful" sizing guide for the future production of clothing lines was produced.

A guide we still use today.

Yes, you read that correctly. The clothing sizes we use to gauge how we feel about our bodies were created by the Department of Agriculture, inspired by the clothing industry and based on 15,000 white women's bodies.

Yes. We too had to pick our jaws up off the ground.

The result was a seed planted deep into our souls that tells us a story—a story that says our bodies "should" all be the same, that we should all be the same size and shape. Our cultural norm demands we be the same, and when we realize that we're not, we feel discouraged and awful about ourselves.

If we're honest, we're often driven by sizes. We might set goals to hit a certain size and then measure our success or failure against that number. Some of us may keep a pair of pants we wore pre-pregnancy, determined to fit into them again. The expectation that we all should be "the same" is harmful and damages us in ways we aren't even aware of.

Until now.

Having Babies Rocks
(but don't rock the family leave boat)

In the American first-world culture, another major "normal" we're faced with is the story of how we're supposed to recover and return to life post-partum. Let's stop for a sec and examine how women and men are treated in the most important moments of creating a family, shall we?

If you live in America, you'll most likely agree family is seen as positive and important. And you'll probably also agree there's a glaring discrepancy between the idea of family and the actionable backing of it.

While our culture endorses the *thought* of kids, it doesn't do much to support *birthing and raising* of kids—a difference between saying and doing. This can be seen dramatically when we compare other cultures to American post-baby cultural norms.

Let's do a little experiment. If you're married, raise your hand if your spouse had paid time off?
(crickets) Thought so.

If you're not married, did your partner get paid time off?
(crickets) Probably not.

If you're single, did your support system get time off to help you?
(crickets) Nah.

The United States is the only country that doesn't currently have a paternity leave law. So while we seem to laud the idea of family, our society doesn't think it's very important to have all hands on deck after baby comes. Based on our cultural norms and even laws, it's believed that partners aren't needed at home in the days and weeks following birth. Vacation time and sick days are saved up as a precious commodity as our due date approaches and then poof, they vanish as quickly as they appeared and we're left to barely survive. *"Family is good in theory but let's not actually support it. Mkay?"* says our culture.

I'll (Sarah) never forget the day my husband returned to work after our first son was born. I was blessed that my mom could come into town and help, and help she did. But there was still that feeling of emptiness and sadness when I stood by the door and watched Steve pull out of the driveway to go to work. It felt very overwhelming and scary. Then came the day, a few days later, when I had to drop my mom off at the airport. Pulling away from the departures curb, I was bawling like a baby. I looked in my rearview at my sleeping baby and said, *"Okay, dude. It's just you and me. We can do this? Right?"* Yeah, it wasn't a statement, it was a question.

Many working moms only get a few weeks off post-partum and A LOT of working moms have anxiety about missing work after having a baby for fear of getting behind and not being seen as valuable.

I (Sarah) had a flexible job, which allowed me to bring Jackson to work with me. This worked well until he started to actually need naps. Then it all quickly fell apart and I found myself incredibly stressed and hiding under my desk to take phone calls for fear of waking my awful napper.

In Mexico, women who have just given birth experience "La cuarentena" or quarantine of 40 days.[iv] During this time moms chill out, recuperate, and bond with their babies. Usually female relatives take command and run all the errands, clean, and cook. Sex is definitely not happening (which seems like a good idea…no?). There are a bunch of do's and don'ts associated with the la cuarentena—such as specific things to eat and not to eat, what women must and must not wear, and definitely no hair washing. (Not sure what that's all about.) Suffice it to say that all over Latin and South America, and really, all over the rest of the world, there are versions of this practice.

In Holland, once a woman has given birth and has returned home, their maternity home care kicks in (covered by insurance).[v] Get this, a nurse shows up for 7 to 10 days and tends to all necessary medical care. Additionally she cooks, cleans, and helps control the flow of post-partum home visitors. Can you imagine having your insurance pay for Mary Poppins who also acts as a bouncer? Sign us up!

The only thing similar to this in the US is a post-partum doula, who acts as a support to the family, can help with laundry, or advise on baby care, sleeping, or feeding. This is usually not covered by insurance however. Womp

Womp. But if you have the budget, it would be a phenomenal help as well as an incredible morale booster.

In my (Sarah's) experience, it wasn't just having my mom around to help me cook and clean and run the house for a week that was the most beneficial. It was having someone who knew what they were doing to coach me and lead me. Having a community of women to surround us and cheer us on while helping with menial tasks is priceless.

It seems our American way of life doesn't really value this whole idea of a set time for family bonding.

I (Jenny) experienced our first-world culture unexpectedly, shortly after the birth of my first daughter. Work called me when Luci was a few weeks old, asking if I would help with a special and time-sensitive project. It was the first of many conflicted moments for me. I was angry and anxious. My anger came from feeling like my promised maternity leave had been violated and I was being taken advantage of, while my anxiety came from my fear of saying no and somehow falling down the chain of influence. After abundant protesting from Franklin, my husband, I said "yes."

That day, as I got dressed, I ran into a rather inconvenient problem. My clothes didn't fit the way they had before. I had boobs I'd never had to deal with, which made my shirts extremely inappropriate. To top it off, my pants were tight and I had to lay on the bed to get them fastened. In the end I paired a nursing tank with a nice sweater and went in. I was called in for a teaching project and as my talk began, so did the hormonal sweating. And then my boobs began to tingle. And my pants were so tight they kept putting pressure on my belly. (I'm sure we all remember the crazy hormones that effect our GI systems, and mine was a special level of crazy that day.) I thought I was destined to have a simultaneous boob and gas explosion.

If there had been a recording of my internal conversation, it would've sounded like this:

Emotional self (said in a Chris Rock type of voice): "Girl, you are in trouble. You're gonna sweat through this cute pink sweater, and worse than that, your upper lip now has a nice shimmer on it."

Logical self: "Remain calm, take a deep breath, and nonchalantly move your hand to your upper lip like you're thinking about what you're gonna say next. Take your pointer finger and slowly wipe the sweat away."

Emotional self: "Keep your arms down!! OMGosh keep your arms down. Whatever you do, don't lift your arms and point at anything. Oh no. Oh no. Is that? Oh yeah. Not now. Those boobs, you gotta stop 'em. Don't think about it. Whatever you do, do not think about nursing right now. Ohhh here comes the tingling. We're in trouble, abort. Wait, what? Now you're gonna throw that one in too? Oh no. I feel that rumbling. It's a bad one too. It's gonna stink. They've been stinkin' all day. You're gonna clear this room. Abort this mission. You cannot do this. You're gonna have pit stains, lip sweat, milk, and nasty gas leakin' all over these poor people. We're going down. We're…going…down…"

I had no business doing that business and yet I felt like I had to in order to not lose any standing with my job. When I was preparing my team to manage without me while I was on maternity leave, I had no idea this would be in my future.

While our nation may, in theory, support women having children, the message it's really sending to us is clear, *"You can have children, just make sure you don't change anything about your life."*

Media's Role

Most of us would agree one of the loudest mouthpieces for messages is media. It's a never-ending, sometimes annoying, most often disruptive noise. A bit like that terrible baby toy your friend bought that goes off in the middle of the night, and no matter how many times you try to throw it away or hide it, it finds it's way back out.

Advertisements on television, billboards, websites, radio, and social media become effective tellers of our first-world story. In fact, according to a new study of media usage and ad exposure by Media Dynamics, Inc., the average adult takes in 360 advertising messages a day.[vi] These mediums tell us what we should feel, how we should think, and how we should act, and are incredibly tricky to identify.

To show just how powerful these messages are, let's try dissecting our own responses to a few. Using the ads below, figure out what the ad makes you think, makes you feel, and how it motivates you to respond.

1. You're walking in the mall and see a print ad for sexy lingerie outside a store. It shows a full wall picture of a woman in her early 20s with larger breasts that reduce into a slim waist and flat stomach. Her shiny legs are slim and smooth. She's dressed in a red and black lacey corset; her blond highlighted hair is layered in tousled curls as she lies on a velvet couch with her back slightly arched off the cushions.

2. As you drive home from the mall you see a car sales billboard. It shows a picture of a couple in their mid-30s. In the passenger seat is a bikini-clad young woman, sitting next to a tanned, shirtless man with muscular arms. They're driving down an empty beachfront road in a sleek black convertible sports car with the top down and surfboards in the backseat.

3. You're cooking dinner and see a television commercial advertising a skin moisturizer. The spokeswoman is a well-known actress in her 20s who is reportedly happily married to another successful actor known for his sex appeal. As she speaks, the camera zooms in close to her skin,

which appears blemish-free and smooth. Her closing line invites you to experience youthful skin.

When I (Jenny) looked at those ads, my biggest feeling was lacking. I felt as though my sex appeal, bedroom attire, and body were inadequate. I felt like a not-fun-old mom and ugly from my blotchy skin. All I could think of was fixing the problem, and to do that I'd certainly need to buy new lingerie, at least clean my car out, and plan a fun outing for me and Franklin where I could get my sexy on in a wild and adventurous way. But first I'd need to stop by an expensive cosmetic store and invest in a really expensive and upgraded face moisturizer.

My (Sarah's) first thought when viewing these ads was "*I don't look like that.*" Followed quickly by some snarky thoughts like "*Aren't corsets torture devices? And someone didn't get the memo about hair extensions being sooo out and the lob being sooo in. Don't women wear cover-ups over their bikinis? I bet that actress doesn't really use this cream, but she sure does peddle the hell out of it, doesn't she?*" My feelings are irritated and slightly envious, which is when I go into snarky/judgment mode. Of course I want skin that smooth and would love to get rid of these bags under my eyes. But since I'm on a super tight budget, I'll just keep Pinteresting the heck outta DIY beauty remedies and hope that rosehips and honey eye cream does the trick.

Stirring our emotions is the real and unsettling purpose of advertisements. The media intentionally manipulates our emotions and has since its inception.

All it takes is logging on to the wonderful world of the internet. We see articles about models who are 8 months pregnant and literally have a six-pack. What? I know. I (Sarah) clicked. I'm a sucker. Then we see images of models strutting their stuff on the catwalk 8 weeks after giving birth, wearing some pretty revealing lingerie, in front of millions of people! Jenny and I agree that it's hard to imagine ourselves in that lingerie in a very dark room with only our husbands! Truth. While modeling is the profession of these women, the investment they and others make in their physical appearance isn't the reality for the majority of us moms.

It's frustrating to turn on the TV and perhaps catch the end of a seasonal lingerie show. In those brief moments the media grabs our hearts, inserts a bunch of negative emotions, and leaves us feeling inadequate and more motivated than ever to buy new products to help alleviate that emotional yuck. Media makers are savvy and are well aware that discontentment drives us. They don't give a flying squirrel if that motivation is healthy or not. The more we expose ourselves to these messages, the more blah we feel. The answers we often pursue satisfy us for a moment and then elude us in the future.

On Demand

Another place where "normal" rears its head in our culture is our addiction to the instantaneous. This one is a sneaky, subversive little ninja, which slinks its way into our hearts, minds, and motives without us even realizing it.

If we want to buy a new album, we go to our media app and have it in hand in seconds. Want to watch a movie? Re-runs? That hard to find obscure flick from college? No worries! We have plenty of on-demand providers to choose from. Before we can even pop a bag of popcorn, we are able to listen to or watch whatever our heart desires.

Our culture normalizes instant: instantly go back to work after having a baby, instantly buy your "you-name-it" and have it show up on your doorstep 24 hours later. Instantly cook a healthy meal and feed it to your happy family for dinner—who for the first time today are all in the same room. Instantly lose weight and get a super model stomach while instantly binge watching a show that makes you think you need to redo your kitchen tomorrow.

We are trained to subconsciously demand instant.

This programming might explain why we get completely discouraged and down in the dumps when weeks or months or even a year or 2 after birth we don't look like we think we should. There is no easy button for the work it will take to feel at peace in our bodies. We get frustrated at our lack of progress, our lack of desire, and feel like everyone else knows something we don't. And the truth is, we all feel this way to varying degrees.

According to Baby Center's New Mom Body Survey: vii

- 61% of new moms said they expected to be back to their pre-pregnancy weight by their baby's first birthday.
- One to two years after giving birth, 86 % of mamas say their belly has not returned to "normal."
- 64% of the mamas taking the survey admitted that their body image has become worse since they became a mama.

Reclaiming our body after kids doesn't happen overnight or even a few overnights...it takes time and requires tremendous patience. Leo Tolstoy wrote, *"The two most powerful warriors are patience and time,"* neither of which are valued in our culture. In fact, they're devalued and become things to demolish. But Tolstoy had it right, they're warriors. When we embrace them and learn to value them, they become invaluable to us and our growth.

Subject or Master?

Now, before we declare total cultural disgust and decide to move our families to a deserted island with no connection to the outside world, it's probably a good idea to recognize that despite these frustrations, our first-world culture is one of our greatest gifts. We, unlike other cultures, have the freedom to filter messages and choose what we believe.

Culture can also be changed, and in America, we've seen this happen in countless generations. Belief systems and values are malleable.

In order to effect change, we must engage and begin to filter our messages and choose differently. When we stop giving our culture the final authority in our lives, culture becomes our subject rather than our master.

When we allow something to be a master in our lives, we give it authority over our thoughts, feelings, and actions. We listen to its voice above all other voices. We place a priority on what it says at a cost to other voices we hear.

Yet when something is our subject we are the ones doing the governing. We rule it and determine its parameters in our lives. We actively decide what we want to believe and then filter those messages accordingly.

It does take work, ya'll. We're not going to lie. It definitely means going against the flow. Media companies estimate we're exposed to several hundred advertisements a day. Did you realize that our favorite TV shows are paid to prominently display products in their episodes? Some of our favorite social media users are paid to promote products, clothing, or the newest most awesome gadget (look for #ad at the end of their finely curated photos.) On top of that we have billboards, radio, magazines, pop-up ads, and the list goes on, all throwing messages our way in hopes of grabbing our attention. Marketing companies know about our consumer fatigue and encourage clients to think creatively.

One marketing website we found says this,[viii]

> *"Of course, most people won't actually recall seeing 10,000 messages. This is because, in order to keep our sanity, we've developed a screening process to ignore most advertising messages. Less than 100 of them make it past our "attention wall" each day. It's simply a matter of self-preservation. This is why you must be creative, memorable, and engaging. Finding an advertising agency or having a creative marketing strategy is a must. If you are not strategic, your efforts will be lost among the multitude of other advertising messages out there."*

Because we're an extremely busy culture, advertisers bank on our inability (or our choice) to filter messages. They rely on our inattention and "stick" messages in our brains that affect us profoundly.

The other day my (Jenny's) kids and I were driving to the store when I overheard Luci, my 6-year-old exclaim, *"Look, Mom, there's the pizza, pizza guy!"* I looked up just as we were driving by a billboard advertising a national pizza company whose commercials include a toga clad guy who says *"pizza, pizza"* at the end of the advertisement. I have no idea where she even heard that or how she knew it, but somehow it had been stuck to her.

47

Anyone know any commercial jingles you wish you didn't? We've got several.

And so, when we find ourselves feeling out of sorts, dissatisfied, or downright not okay with our lives, it's so crucial for us to figure out if these messages are our master, or our subject.

Emotional Awareness

I (Jenny) wasn't that emotive until I had my first baby, which came as somewhat of a shock to my close family. I remember coming downstairs from nursing Luci during the first week of her life with joyful tears in my eyes and my mom exclaiming, "*What's wrong with you?*"
As a new mom I had what I call "big" feelings. I felt a lot of different emotions and experienced them deeply (almost crazy deep). While this was a new experience for me, I enjoyed feeling more and realized these emotions told me a few things. My nightly tears and anxiety told me I was tired and felt overwhelmed with a colicky baby. My anger at people ringing the doorbell—while Luci was sleeping—told me I was more concerned with her well-being than being nice. And my overwhelming joy when I saw that sweet baby in the morning told me I enjoyed being a mom tremendously.

My emotions were, and still are, the gauge of my inner thoughts. To realize when we've become the subject of messages rather than the master requires us to chase our emotions. Asking ourselves what we're feeling and why we're feeling it allows us to get to the heart of the matter. Most often, tension, dissatisfaction, disgust, fear, or any other emotions have a belief attached to them that we might not be aware of.

In order to become aware of the way we're being influenced by media, we must become informed consumers. This requires us to understand when our emotions are being manipulated.

According to an article in *Psychology Today*:

> *"It is important to distinguish healthy social influence from psychological manipulation. Healthy social influence occurs between most people, and is part of the give and take of constructive relationships. In psychological manipulation, one person is used for the benefit of another. The manipulator deliberately creates an imbalance of power, and exploits the victim to serve his or her agenda.[ix]"*

While it may sound extreme to label commercials, billboards, or magazine ads as manipulators, we believe that's what they are. Their agenda is to exploit our emotions and motivate us towards action—action that often involves consuming and promoting their products. As we watch, see, and listen to their messages we can take control by pausing to recognize what emotions are being elicited and re-establish ourselves in the truth

49

rather than blindly accepting what they're communicating.

When my (Sarah's) son started taking an archery class this year, I was surprised to learn on day 1 that Jackson is left-eye dominant even though he's right handed with other things. Since lefties have to use a left-handed bow when they shoot, at the start of class Jackson has to grab the correct bow for his lefty-ness.

Last week—the 8th week of class—we had only been at the class for about 20 minutes when Jackson suddenly appeared in the waiting area with tears in his eyes. Immediately I could sense something was "off" but didn't know what it was. I asked Jackson, "*What happened?*" He replied, "*Nothing.*" I pushed a bit further. "*Why are you crying?*" Jackson said he wasn't sure. I was baffled. This was very out of character for my child. I asked him if someone said something to him, or touched him? Nope. Nothing happened. Jackson said his tummy hurt and asked if we could leave.

Later at home that night I was trying to gently prod him to figure out the cause of his emotion—clearly he was feeling fine since upon getting home he was outside running around and playing. Jackson stuck to his story about his tummy ache. I was feeling concerned and worried and decided at bedtime to broach the subject one last time. Jackson said, "*Do you promise you won't get mad?*" My heartbeat quickened, my imagination was on overload, I swallowed and pasted a smile on my face and said, "*Of course not, hunny!*" I imagined the worst things.

Jackson simply said, "*You know how I shoot left-handed?
Well, I grabbed the right-handed bow.*" Still smiling, I said,
"*So you grabbed the wrong bow and that's the reason you were
crying?*" Jackson explained further, "*I was shooting with it
and thought that my class would laugh and make fun of me and I
didn't know what to do. I felt embarrassed.*" After talking for
a few more minutes and drilling down to the root, I
discovered that Jackson was scared. Scared of being
embarrassed. Aside from feeling immensely relieved
about what Jackson was telling me, I was pretty stunned.

Somewhere along the way, Jackson had picked up and
bought into this belief that his class was aware of his
every move and was waiting for him to screw up so they
could laugh at him. This belief took him captive and was
responsible for us hightailing it home after only 20
minutes at class. The truth in this situation is that
everyone is focused on his/her own bow and arrows.
They aren't even paying attention to Jackson because
they're focused on their own targets.

This whole predicament opened the door to a sweet
conversation about the truth of the situation and I gave
Jackson some examples about how I've messed up, made
assumptions, or believed things that weren't true. The
moral of the story: when we encounter these feelings, we
get to the root of it, look at it, acknowledge it, brush it
off, and move on.

Asking questions (especially the question "why") is an
effective way to get to the heart of the untruths that we
buy into on a daily basis. It's a lot easier to do this with
our kids than it is to do with ourselves, yet it's vitally

important to becoming the masters rather than the subject. We take back the power from the emotional manipulators (in this case media messages) by choosing to be an active participant, to question, to persist, to drill down to the core of our feelings, and in doing so, to filter out the unhelpful messages that are setting us back.

What You Have

In Dr. Seuss's *Horton Hears a Who*, a tiny village runs the risk of being destroyed. In order to be rescued they all must make enough noise so that together, their tiny voices will be heard.

"We've GOT to make noises in greater amounts! So, open your mouth, lad! For every voice counts!"

As we learn to recognize the stories that lead us to unhealthy pursuits, we *can* influence this ginormous cultural ship. While your one voice may not be heard from the deck of the boat, all our voices, joined together, can be heard.

With each purchase, we speak with our money. With each social media post, we speak with our social influence. With each conversation we have with our children, we speak with our parental authority.

But it takes the whole village. Making noise at the same time. At the same thing. For the same reason.

So whaddaya say? How will you begin to leverage your influence—and sister, you've got some—in order to change the story for future generations about women's bodies after baby?

Recap

- ✓ There are two major areas that can cause us to struggle with our post-baby bodies: our culture and our relationships.
- ✓ The US Agricultural Dept. set our clothing size standards. Be careful what and who you base your self-image off of.
- ✓ Our culture supports family but doesn't really promote family. The United States is the only first-world country that doesn't have any partner leave laws.
- ✓ The mouthpiece for our culture is media and it's hard to get away from it. It's a powerful communication tool that can lead us to feeling discontentment.
- ✓ We're becoming addicted to instant everything, which leads us to depression or intense discouragement when we aren't where we think we "should" be. (Or leads us to pride, which isn't helpful either.)
- ✓ Our culture can either be our master or our subject.

Action Steps
Journal or Discuss

✖ To start this chapter's action steps, spend a few minutes thinking/journaling what you're currently feeling about your post-partum body and mind.

✖ Okay, now we've got a challenge for you and you might wanna ask a friend to join you.

We challenge you to a 3-day media fast. Pick your primary form of media intake (Facebook, TV, Instagram, the newspaper (remember those?) and disengage with it for 3 days. 3 full days.

After the 3 days are over, check back in for your next step. Ready and go.

✖ Welcome back. Now that you've experienced a media fast, spend some time reflecting on how you currently feel about your post-baby body. Different? Worse? Better? The same? There are no right answers. The goal is to experiment with this idea that our media heavily influences our contentment.

3

Being At War With Oneself

I feel guilty having an unloving relationship with my body after the resilience, strength and loyalty it has demonstrated to me on giving me my beautiful baby—makes me feel so shallow having these thoughts knowing I have a healthy baby.

DEE, mom of 1

This morning I (Jenny) sat on the couch taking the sacred first sip of coffee, only to have Franklin run naked out of the bedroom and begin frantically searching through the pile of unfolded laundry on the couch. As he rummaged he mumbled, *"I don't have any clean underwear."* I stopped sipping, looked at him, and said, *"Nope, I didn't wash them yesterday. I didn't know you didn't have any clean."* Exasperated, he shot back, *"I only have seven pairs, you should know I needed some washed."* At this point, I was convinced his attitude had ruined the taste of my coffee and I snapped back, *"I'm not a mind reader. You should tell me."* And with that, our day was off to a great start.

I've noticed a pattern in my marriage that can be summed up in one word: "blame." When something goes wrong, our default is to find someone or something other than ourselves to blame. It's just easier. If it's someone else's issue, then I'm absolved of any responsibility that may require me to slow down, be thoughtful, and *gasp*, apologize.

While last chapter had tough moments, let's admit, it was kinda easy. It's easy to blame our culture and media for the discontentment we experience with our bodies. What's harder is to look within ourselves, to slow down, to be thoughtful about our feelings, and maybe even apologize to ourselves.

In this day and age especially, taking responsibility for our own feelings, our own "stuff," is counter-cultural. And while working together to help influence our culture is important, it can't be our only focus. To experience the most powerful growth, we're required to spend time taking ownership for the part we play in our own discontentment.

To help us gain perspective, we need to examine our relationships' beginning, primarily, with the one we have with ourselves. For the next few chapters, we'll focus our energy on these areas where we can make a major difference. We'd like to keep it relatively simple by looking at "the Big Four" relationships many of us have:

→ Relationship with ourselves
→ Relationship with our partners
→ Relationship with our kids
→ Relationship with our friends

There's an "I" in Discontentment

Elizabeth, a first-time mom, shared with us the first time she realized she felt conflicted about her body after giving birth: *"Going out for the first time, and I couldn't find a coat that I could zip up. A coat. I own 19 of them (don't judge). And none of them would zip up. That's when I sat down and cried."*

We've all been there, haven't we? We sit down and ugly cry not because of what just happened, but because of all of it. And yet, our first-world culture demands we live a fast-paced, multi-dimensional life—which excludes us from slowing down for personal reflection. Just about the moment we get self-reflective and thoughtful, a kid finds their way into the closet where we've hidden ourselves and asks for a snack and any chance of healing is buried in a peanut butter sandwich.

And so, for this chapter, we're pushing the pause button because it's crucial for your health.

When our inner thoughts and feelings are—for a majority of the time—in a positive place, we're more available to our partners, friends and children. We're more joyful. We're happier. We're more patient. We're more generous. We're more because we have more to give. This more, is only accessible to us through the medium of hard work.

Contentment starts with us.

Power of the Past

It's funny to think about having a relationship with ourselves and yet, for many of us, there's a constant dialogue that plays in our heads of self-praise or self-condemnation. Changing that inner closed captioning feed requires us to do a couple things; spend time in the past while acknowledging the present and fighting our fear.

For me (Jenny) being outside and having mental and physical time to myself is golden. I especially love to run on trails in the woods where no one is around to hear me talk to myself or sit on a log for a good old-fashioned cry. It's my space of freedom. A few summers ago as I was running, I rounded a corner and fell on a slick spot—it was a brutal fall where I made strange childbirth type sounds when I hit the ground.

In that moment, all I could do was roll over on my back and take a deep breath. I knew if I wanted to get back to my car, which was miles and miles away, I had to ignore the gaping wounds.

Hours later, I ended up in the doctor's office to have my injuries cleaned. The scrubbing was the worst part. There was so much debris embedded in it that it took extra cleaning and a rather large bandage.

By ignoring the injury and finishing the run, I made the healing process longer and more painful. I finished and made it back to my car, which is what I needed to do at the time. But at some point, I had to face the deep wound and have it cleaned. If left untreated, it would've infected my entire body.

There are wounds many of us carry in regards to our bodies that are infecting our relationships. We know this is a scary and painful door for us to open. It requires honesty, vulnerability, and coming to terms with the messiness of our past. It also has the biggest potential for transformation. Win this one, and we can win them all. Abandoning this one means a never-ending battle on other relational fronts.

We're sure there are positive moments in your life regarding your contentment. Sadly, we suspect there might be more negative moments etched into our hearts and minds. The statements someone made about our body or the way someone looked at us can come flooding back with little help.

Sometimes we have to ignore pain to survive a tough season. There are moments when we don't have the luxury of slowing down to process our feelings and have to be tough to press on. But at some point it's important for us to revisit these painful moments and find healing.

Looking back allows us to process wounds differently than we did the first time. This practice lets us experience a full healing, so that our lives are no longer influenced by unhealthy thinking.

What's Your Story?

In order to move us closer to our personal goals of contentment, we need an honest assessment of how we feel about ourselves and why. Let's jump back to our survey that we mentioned in Chapter 1—the survey that hundreds of women responded to, and that catapulted and validated the need for this book. We wanted our survey to capture thoughts and feelings, which required open-ended questions. As we received responses from moms, we were surprised to get additional comments of gratitude for facilitating a cathartic experience. Telling our story can be healing and insightful.

We'd like to invite you to share this experience and take our survey. So grab a pen and a cup of something nice (no judgment if that means coffee and Baileys) and spend some time reflecting on your post-baby body journey.

Post-Baby Body Survey Questions

1. How did you feel about your body **before** pregnancy?

2. How did you feel about your body **during** pregnancy?

3. How did you feel about your body within the few months **after** giving birth?

4. Do you feel content with the way you body looks and functions right now, physically?

5. Do you feel content with how your body functions sexually?

6. What's your favorite thing about your body after baby?

7. If you could change one thing about your body today, what would it be?

8. What's one word that describes your relationship with your body right now?

9. What does your partner think about your post-baby body?

10. Is your partner content with their body?

You still with us? Hopefully that was more cathartic than painful. But we have to tell you, we can't stop there; we have to go a little deeper. Our current reality is most often shaped by our past experiences because history can subconsciously affect our thoughts and feelings.

We'd like to now invite you to spend time creating what we call a contentment line. This is a physical representation of your journey with your body. Next, you'll see a chart broken into 8 different life stages. You'll also notice on the left column, the numbers 10-1. Spend a few minutes thinking through how you felt and what you thought about your body during each of these life stages. Then, rank them in terms of 10 representing the highest level of bodily contentment and 1 being the lowest level of bodily contentment by putting a big dot in the column. Once you're done, connect each dot in order to see your contentment line.

Your Contentment Line

Rank	Child	Pre-teen	High School	20s	30s	40s	50s	60s
1								
2								
3								
4								
5								
6								
7								
8								
9								
10								

Now, looking back on your contentment line, spend some time reflecting on the following questions.

1. When were your high points?
2. How often do you remember these high points?
3. When were your low points?
4. How often in your daily living do you remember these low points?
5. Which do you spend more time reflecting on, the highs or lows?
6. What feelings do the low points evoke in you right now?
7. Is this low point affecting other areas of your life?
8. Is this a wound you'd like to heal?

With these personal reflections we each have a starting point, a place from which we'll grow. Our hope at the end of this book is that you'll be able to say you moved your contentment number. Whether you're at a 1 or at a 5, we want you to move closer to a 10, even if that means by .01. **Any forward movement is growth.**

Embracing, rather than shunning our emotions, whatever they may be, is our first step in winning the battle within. Feeling them, processing them, and moving through them allows us to heal, which is a form of growth. It also allows us to hold onto the good and root ourselves in the truth while tossing the lies.

Recap

- ✓ The relational battle starts with us. It's in our own hearts and minds.
- ✓ We're multi-dimensional and multi-conflicted! We're super proud of what our bodies have done and all they've been through AND we're unhappy and dissatisfied and sometimes, disgusted with them.
- ✓ There's value in looking back in our lives because it helps us gain perspective and healing so we can move closer to contentment.
- ✓ Growth is measured by movement. It doesn't matter how much or how little, forward progress is growth.

Action Steps
Journal or Discuss

- ✂ Our action steps today were the body after baby survey and the contentment line on the previous pages.

4

Bodily Changes

It is a constant struggle between logic and vanity. I knew I had just grown and given birth to a child, which is a major experience for a body to have gone through. I knew nothing would be the same. But then vanity came into play when I was still wearing maternity jeans, and nothing fit.

ELIZABETH, mom of 1

I (Sarah) often reflect on the process of pregnancy. The minute we see those double pink lines, our life changes. Suddenly our priorities are different. We start drinking more water; we cut out caffeine and Google the hell out of everything. "*What can I eat while pregnant?*" We want someone to tell us the must dos and must not dos. Suddenly we have to pee every five seconds. We are aghast that we're unexpectedly out of breath when we climb the smallest set of stairs.

Basically the 10 months that pregnancy spans brings a lot of change. Some of the change is so subtle we're oblivious to it. The rest of it is like a buffalo stampede. Regardless, we're changing.

Many of us don't struggle with bodily contentment through pregnancy most likely because other people don't seem to care if we've gained a little or a lot of weight and typically keep the unhelpful comments to themselves. (Except for a few idiots out there…oh the stories we could all tell.)

For those 10 months some of us binge read books on bringing our baby home and what to expect from them the first year of life. While that's necessary, we're neglecting another important element: ourselves. None of us are thinking through what OUR first year might be like. Our priorities, sleep, shower habits and the fit of our clothes all change. It ALL changes. Heraclitus, a Greek philosopher known for many maxims said, *"There is nothing permanent except change."* True that Heraclitus, true that.

Inner contentment requires us to acknowledge our changing present reality. Instead of crying about it, Jenny and I have decided these life movements and changes might be more freedom producing when viewed with acceptance and humor. For this chapter we'll embrace this truth and turn against the "normal" idea that change should be feared or hated and instead we're gonna laugh. A lot.

Looking in the Mirror

Post-partum is complex. It doesn't just hit our emotional insides; we also have to deal with the ever-changing physical transformations. One boob is now higher than the other, what started our sex engine before now makes it sputter. Shoot, our feet might even be a different size. There's movement (lots of freakin' movement) most of us experience with how our body looks and operates and the crazy part is, everyone's shift is different. (Shift....not shit...although that can change too.)

So with that in mind, we're gonna let you in on some of the ways our (Sarah and my) bodies have changed. Then we're gonna throw in a few stories from other mamas. Why? Because getting vulnerable is helpful. We seriously can't make this stuff up. Our changes might be different than yours, but most often we can relate to each other because the feelings they produce in us give us lots and lots of common ground.

Let's start with our stomachs. I (Jenny) had no idea it can take anywhere from 4-8 weeks or more for our organs to settle back into place and our uterus to shrink back to its pre-baby size. A new mom can expect to lose 10-12 lbs. from delivering a baby, placenta, and fluid. The rest takes time. It's even recommended that women not diet until at least 8 weeks post-partum. Age, genetics, and even the position of the baby can have a profound impact on this process. Your post-partum stomach is like your fingerprints; no two are alike and beautifully and uniquely yours.

I never had stretch marks with my first baby. Then came Levi, my second, and he decided he wanted to stay curled like a basketball the entire last trimester. Now, several years post-partum, I have a stomach that looks like a deflated tire, despite me being a very healthy weight. And unless I want to pay money to have surgery and get a tummy tuck, it'll stay with me until I see Jesus. No matter how much I workout, eat clean, or don't eat at all, this stomach will continue to look this way. The stretch marks were a gift Levi decided I needed. Thanks, son. You cute little jerk.

Another discovery some of us may have to navigate are the new sounds our bodies might make. Oh yes, we said sounds.

I (Sarah) went to prenatal yoga religiously when I was pregnant with our first. It was a gift to myself and I loved it. When the yoga studio sent me an email about its "mommy and me" yoga class after I gave birth, I was pumped to do that too. I couldn't wait to sign up.

Then I experienced my first vart. You with me, mama? A vagina fart. Some of you may call it a "queef" or "plain disgusting." Take your pick and keep truckin'.

I was at home doing some stretching exercises a couple months after our son was born. I shifted positions and BAM, a sound exploded out of my vagina like crashing thunder. I was shocked. I was mortified. I was terrified. What in the world was *that*? I wanted to run for cover.

Instead, I ran to my computer and promptly Googled it and then swiftly called my mom, laughing and crying my eyes out. I knew at that moment I would never be caught dead in yoga class again. I was banishing myself. For life.

Even though I knew that Google recognized it as a legit post-partum "thing," I still felt like a freak of nature. I mean, how are there even post-partum yoga classes if this is a "thing"? Are earplugs provided? Yoga class with bumping bass track?

I still don't know the answer to that because I never went back. But if any of you have insight on this, please let me know! I'm dying of curiosity.

Being naturally curious, I researched the mechanics of a vart and I'm sure you're dying to know why this happens. Put on your medical coat, here goes:

→ Our vagina is a tube and at one end is our uterus and at the other end is the part that goes to the outside, where our external lady parts reside.

→ For 10 months we've had a baby who has been putting the pressure on us and all our bits and pieces.

→ After that, we push a baby out of it or have surgeons who get the baby out for us, and regardless of the birthing process, there's pressure involved.

→ Our vajayjays are probably a bit more, "stretched" than they were before and our bladder is often squished by the uterus falling into it due to muscle atrophy. They beckon air to come in and hang out.

→ But what comes in must go out, so when we switch positions, bam. The air rushes out, like hordes of tweens leaving a Taylor Swift concert.

→ My lady, you just varted.

To my credit, in researching this issue, I have realized that the "yoga queef" is indeed a real phenomenon with proper name. And in addition to that, my husband has also come to realize that varts are the price of doing "the wild monkey dance" together. We have since become comfortable with these random bursts of air, much like one becomes deaf to Navy jets flying overhead or trains rumbling down the tracks in the backyard. It has just become part of my married, post-partum, sexy time landscape.

Once again, it's evident we all change and ain't none of it the same. See? It's fun to hear about other people's bodily change. It helps us find contentment with our change.

Shall we keep going?

I (Jenny) was super naïve about my bodily changes. Before I had my first, I realized my due date was such that I could give birth to Luci and then run two of my favorite half marathons, 12 weeks later. With 6 weeks to train, I decided it was the perfect plan to take back my body!

No one told me. No one told me that could've possibly been the dumbest thing I'd ever decided to do. (Sarah note: Where was I, Jenny? I would have told you!) The Cincinnati half came first. I was nursing every 2-3 hours and was a pretty good milk truck. I timed it out, and as we parked close to the starting line, I sat in the backseat and pumped. I then jumped out of the car and made it to the start just as the gun went off. I was somewhat okay until mile 6. And that's when 2 things simultaneously began happening. First, I began to have serious hip discomfort and lots of pressure down below. I thought my insides were going to fall out. I thought, any moment, in my running shorts, my uterus, vagina, and whatever else is up in there would come spilling out. Second, I began peeing in my pants…a constant stream that couldn't be stopped. I tried squeezing whatever was left in my body, hoping desperately something would listen as my brain screamed, "*Shut it off!*"

But it didn't. Nothing listened and nothing worked. Praise Jesus it was raining that day. When I finished I made a beeline for the car because I thought my boobs were going to explode. I remember sitting in the backseat, listening to the loud waa-waa-waa sound of my pump, smelling like pee.

Six days later I ran another half marathon. This time, I really believed I wasn't going to make it. My hips and back weren't fully recovered from the strains of pregnancy. While my lungs could make 13.1 miles, my body wasn't there yet. I cried. I ran and cried. Fortunately, I wore bike shorts. The standard, sewn-in pad, meant to help cushion my butt during a long ride, absorbed the pee that continued to freely flow.

I remember feeling so sad and angry with my body. I felt like it betrayed me. Lied to me. Let me down. No matter how much I commanded it to "*Work like it did before*," or told it to "*Be tough*," it was tired and needed me to give it the time to heal.

Sigh. If only our bodies listened to what we told them. We'd be good. We'd avoid all bodily changes. Nothing would take our contentment. Period. (Speaking of periods. That first one after birth was like a volcano erupting for the first time. Dang.)

Let's chat for a sec about our wide hips. Yeah. That happens. Think about it: there's really no way a watermelon can pass through the eye of a needle without some adjustments. We're also sure our jeans don't lie. For some mamas, clothes fit differently after having kids. I (Jenny) decided instead of buying bigger jeans, to use rubber bands wrapped through the buttonhole of my jeans and stretched around the actual button, would suffice as an appropriate "expander." My budget and my jeans had zero wiggle room.

Interestingly, lots of moms we spoke with also mentioned a seismic shift in their proportions after birth. It seems that some of our beautiful luscious breasts migrated south to join our already robust and roly-poly midsections while our bootylicious asses started drooping like a wilted flower neglected in the hot sun, begging for a sip of cool water. And ladies, this phenomenon is happening all over the world. And frankly, for me (Sarah), as an A cup pre-birth to a C cup while breastfeeding, to a NO cup now…it's a bitter pill to swallow.

Sounds like an old country song we know. Ready for verse two?

Managing Change:
Experiences from Real-Life Moms

Vicki, mama of 1, experienced a profound moment after the birth of her baby where she looked at herself in the mirror and didn't recognize the body looking back at her. "*I ended up having a cesarean delivery, which was not the plan. It was the next morning and my husband walked me to the shower so I could get cleaned up. I saw in that horrible lighting exactly what [my body] looked like. In pregnancy the changes are slow. After [our baby] came, the change was instant. I never thought I would have to have so much help to get in the shower and clean myself. It was the overwhelming feeling that nothing looked like I'd seen it look before.*"

Vicki essentially went from having to pee every five seconds when pregnant to an emergency C-section and needing her hubby's help to go pee. It was a shocker.

Vicki remembered, *"I would look down and wonder what even happened. EVERY part of my body looked and felt utterly broken, unrecognizable."*

While Vicki was adjusting to the first few weeks and months of mothering, she was also healing (physically and emotionally) while getting to know and love her body as it is now. *"[My body] feels like a gift. Like it's been emptied out sacrificially. I'm finding beauty in there. Physically, I now look at my strong legs and love them. We've got miles to cover and places to go with [our son]. Bring it on."*

And there's more. Here are some changes from other mamas:

> *"After years of fertility drugs, early miscarriages, and finally two full term babies in less than two years, I look at my body as a machine! We went to war and came back with a few dents and mechanical issues, but we did it! Maybe I will never be the media's idea of sexy or pretty or even "healthy," but I know my body is awesome. Scars, extra skin, and the occasional leaky bladder won't change that!"*
> —Adrian, Mom of 2

> *"I have 15% body fat and can't fill the smallest cup size available. I can do amazing things with my body, but I don't feel sexy. Just really powerful. I want to get the dainty side of me back. But moms aren't dainty anyway. I think that part of me is gone and I need to embrace the "utility" version of myself."*
> —Amanda, mom of 2

"I feel content with how my body is functioning (making milk, recovering from birth). I feel good about how I look. I've got a lot of fat still, but my appreciation for my body is greater. With this comes a grace I guess–I'm not as hard on myself about my looks, it all happens in its sweet time, now it's time for enjoying." —Annalisa, mom of 1

"Breastfeeding has wrecked my boobs and I could scare some people if they saw me without a bra! I weigh the same as pre-babies but my body looks totally different. My belly will always have stretch marks and be rather play-dough-ish. I don't expect to look 22 anymore, though, and I'm able to give grace to the imperfectness of it."
—Carrie, mom of 3

Knowing we've each experienced and are experiencing change can make us feel less alone and more united. When I (Jenny) see another mama at the park, it's like we're in this secret club together. My body and her body and your body are super hero bodies (despite what our culture thinks.) We created, housed, and birthed a human life. Our bodies are reliable and capable, doing what they've been created to do.

Sharing our current reality helps us acknowledge our journey and give it proper respect. The opposite of respect is insult, and insult brings shame. When we're not capable of being honest in our current reality of change, we subconsciously shame ourselves into believing our body is "bad." That's the destructive inner dialog we're here to heal.

We believe our bodies even deserve honor. This honor requires us to embrace what they've done and be grateful. **Gratitude leads to deeper contentment**. An attitude of thankfulness is one of our most powerful weapons against discontentment. We stop pursuing "normal" when we center our energy and focus on appreciating our bodies.

We do understand it's hard to be grateful for some of the changes that bring us to places of negative emotions. If you're not sure where to start on this gratitude path, we will give you some direction in our journal section. In the meantime, mama, laugh away at all the crazy, beautiful changes we all experience. Laugh in your bathroom alone and laugh while walking out to the pool with your girlfriends. It is crazy. Crazy good.

Recap

✓ Our bodies change because of having babies and because we are also aging.
✓ Saggy boobs
✓ Deflated tire-looking stomachs
✓ Stretch marks
✓ Varts
✓ Peeing in the pants
✓ No one escapes motherhood unscathed in some area, be it physical, mental, or emotional.

✓ Gratitude for our bodies and all they've done for us (and our kids) leads to deeper contentment and also gives us a link to all the other super hero women's bodies.

Action Steps

Journal or Discuss

- Let's spend some time being grateful. It may be the last thing you really want to do, but gratitude is a choice that pays a big return. Spend a few minutes thinking through your journey into Motherhood. List 3 things you're grateful your body has done for you.
  1.
  2.
  3.

- Now, spend a few minutes writing down one or two post-partum body changes that make you laugh.
  1.
  2.

- Next, list a few changes that make you feel anything <u>other than</u> joy or contentment.
  1.
  2.
  3.

✂ And now a big challenge. We want you to share these things with another mama. Specifically, we want you to share the few changes that keep you from experiencing contentment. And we want you to ask your mom friend if they've experienced any of those things too.

✂ Then come back and spend some time reflecting on that experience. How did it feel to share your contentment obstacle? Scary? Liberating? How did your mama friend respond? How did that make you feel?

We're not alone, friends, and there's nothing new under the sun[x]. You are not a freak of nature. You are beautiful and unique and amazing. Let's take the time and energy to be vulnerable and share with other mamas this journey we are on. We'll surprise ourselves with the fine company we're surrounded by and the incredible vulnerability we receive in return.

5

The Fear-ocious Fight

I must not fear. Fear is the mind-killer. Fear is the little-death that brings total obliteration. I will face my fear. I will permit it to pass over me and through me. And when it has gone past I will turn the inner eye to see its path. Where the fear has gone there will be nothing. Only I will remain.

FRANK HERBERT - *Dune*

Well, friends, we hope your hearts are full of gratitude cause we're gonna need that to help us walk through this heavy topic. As we keep battling our inner thinking, we have to address one of the biggest obstacles of all, fear. We're not talking afraid of the dark fear; we're talking anxiety producing, depression driving, binge-eating fear. And this is one struggle we can't afford to lose.

It might seem weird to talk about fear in regards to our post-baby body. However, for a majority of moms, it's one of the biggest contributors of discontentment. We can't find peace when we're apprehensive and our "normal" is riddled with fear. Stand in a checkout line at the store and you'll see magazines telling you to be fearful and then offering you the solution to satiate your fear.

Have weight gain? Read our dieting tips. Think your partner isn't sexually fulfilled? Read our sex advice. Have an outdated wardrobe? Read our fashion suggestions. Need tips on how to be sexy? Download our pole dancing video.

These concerns aren't even on our mental radar but when we read them, well yeah, we worry. In that brief moment, we worry about our weight, fear our partners are gonna leave us for a better version of ourselves, hate the clothes we have on, and oddly feel compelled to learn to dance and buy new lingerie. Brilliant marketing—create a problem that doesn't really exist (a lie) and then offer, for a small amount of money, to fix the fake problem. Fear is a powerful motivator.

I (Jenny) actually fell for this once and bought a pole dancing video. I threw it away after my father-in-law found it on our video rack. I wasn't very good at it anyways, I just laughed the whole time, and my sexy face looked like duck face.

Fear is so sneaky we often label it as anxiety or depression or addiction or insecurity. But we're here to expose it for what it is, an a-hole—no one wants to look at one, but everyone has one.

Here's our "fear" reality. According to the CDC and the National Health and Nutrition Examination Surveys, 2005–2008: [xi]

- 11% of Americans aged 12 years and over, take anti- depressant medication.
- Women are more likely than guys to take anti-depressants.
- 6 out of 10 people taking antidepressants have taken it for 2 years or longer.

Researchers at the Anxiety and Depression Association of America have found:[xii]

- Anxiety disorders are extremely common. In fact, 18% of all Americans struggle with it…ya'll, that's over 40 million of us.

- Like depression, us ladies are twice as likely as men to have anxiety.

Just reading these stats hits home for me (Jenny.) Back in 2009 I started having panic attacks that were debilitating. I would wake up in the middle of the night feeling and believing I was gonna die. Most often it would result in me puking and not sleeping. I would go to work and sleep because I wasn't sleeping at night. It started affecting all areas of my life and for this stay in control girl, it was terrible.

After exhausting all of my ideas and taking way too much melatonin (and Benadryl and alcohol), I found myself crying in the doctor's office. That day he gave me 30 days of anti-anxiety medicine and sent me to therapy. I was at a new low walking out of that office.

Eight years later I now understand my anxiety was a result of ignored and unprocessed fear. During that season I had started a new job and was super fearful of sucking at it. Franklin had also taken a job working second shift in the ER and I was alone at night. To top it off, I experienced a traumatic event that left me fearful of both emotional and physical pain.

Instead of seeking the help of my community or a trained therapist, I just ran. I tried to run out my anxiety and ended up making it worse. I kept shoving it in and it kept spilling out in the form of terrible panic attacks.

In therapy, I learned how to recognize and respond to my fears in a healthy way. Fortunately, this stopped the emotional leaking. Occasionally, when life gets crazy and I forget to spend time meditating, fear creeps back in and I experience increased anxiety. I'm still fighting this battle and most likely always will. Stuffing and suppressing my feelings seems to be my default. My hope is that I'm getting better at processing my fears and keeping them from getting to the point where I'm experiencing full-blown panic attacks.

We all face fear. It's part of our emotional makeup and can actually keep us safe when it's directed at legit dangerous things. But—as with anything—that which can be helpful can also be harmful. Fear, triggered by false beliefs, can be extremely destructive to our minds. It can stop us in our tracks, leaving us stuck.

In the next pages, we want to spotlight 3 fears that post-partum moms might feel. We'll look at the fear of being undesirable, the fear of inadequacy, and the fear of vulnerability. Then we're going to tackle exactly how to overcome them.

Fear of Being Undesirable

"The skin on my stomach is gross. I don't let my husband see me without a shirt on. I fear I will never feel comfortable naked or in a bikini ever again." Megan, mama of 2 kiddos.

Anyone ever had those thoughts and feelings? Yeah. We have. What Megan said is an incredibly vulnerable confession of a post-partum mama. One of the most common fears we all face is that our post-partum bodies will no longer be physically desired.

The quote about beauty being in the eye of the beholder is confusing. What happens when I behold my image in the mirror and I hate it? Is what we see what others see? Is it what our partners see? (Even if they say they see something different.) Because we've changed, we're not sure about the reality of what anyone is seeing. This causes tension and conflict and starts a negative cycle.

Here's how this works. When I (Sarah) feel ugly and therefore believe I'm not desirable, I physically move away from Steve. I jokingly shimmy out of his arms and swat his hands away. He then most often feels like I'm rejecting him, feels hurt, and stops pursuing me. Which feeds into my belief that I'm undesirable. Which leads me to feel deeper shame and push him away more, which leads to him feeling more hurt and pursuing less, which ultimately leaves both of us hurt and disconnected. See? It's like riding a terrible carnival ride that never stops. It's crazy how so much movement can never lead to a place of contentment—just an island of disconnection (with scary clowns).

But, when I believe I'm beautiful, strong, and healthy, I welcome Steve's affections. My choice to say "Yes, I'm desirable, dammit" leads me to saying "Yes" to Steve. This makes him feel connected to me, which makes him pursue me more passionately. This bolsters my feelings of being desired and wanted. This allows me to embrace his pursuit as he pursues me more. This results in both of us feeling wanted and connected. Yeah for relational growth!

Being desired isn't solely contingent on our looks. (If it is, then we're all lying to our kids when we tell them inner beauty is as important as outward.) If we take the emotion out of it, we all can identify experiences where we've desired to connect with people for reasons other than their looks.

I (Jenny) fought against this fear after the birth of our first. I had some serious vaginal trauma with the birth of Luci. My healing was slow and painful. The first time Franklin and I tried to have post-partum sex I ended up crying and having a panic attack. Super sexy. For the next year certain sex positions that had once been our favorites were off limits. Even more upsetting, was sex started with me smearing Lidocaine all over my vagina so I wouldn't feel the pain. Since I physically couldn't do some of his favorite things, I believed he would begin to hate sex with me, fall in love with another woman who was more desirable than me and have an affair, leaving both Luci and me alone. I just knew it was inevitable. I was doomed to be abandoned because I couldn't have sex the same way as pre-baby.

Sounds illogical, irrational, and silly, right? It does. But man were those feelings real. It took a good year for things to return to functioning (but just a few months to realize Franklin likes all sex positions.) Haha. For real.

When we turn on the logical sides of our brains, we can see our fear of being undesirable isn't always based on reality. As we see this, we begin to choose truth over anxiety. Saying "yes" is a choice. It's not pretending. It's not ignoring. It's a willful changing of the mind. The more we choose to say "yes" to valuing ourselves, and to seeing the truth of our own worth, the more we allow ourselves to believe we are beautiful, valuable, and amazing.

While the feeling of fear can be real, the reason for feeling undesirable is as fake (and ugly) as your grandma's lawn gnome.

Fear of Inadequacy

Think back to the generation or two before us. Mothers were most often defined as homemakers, called each other from phones stuck to a wall (with a cord), and watched televisions that had to be manually changed. Hand-written letters were a primary form of communication, and a kid on a bike delivered the daily news. It was a vastly different world than our on-demand and fast-paced reality. However, we're pretty confident that even back then, women still struggled with inadequacy.

The fear of inadequacy is a timeless fear *but* the way in which we define "adequate" is really dependent upon our environment. As we've already mentioned, we have quite a barrage of wanted and unwanted information at our fingertips in seconds, which feeds our natural tendency to feel like we don't measure up, especially in the realm of motherhood.

Inadequacy is defined as incompleteness or defectiveness[xiii]. If we have fears of inadequacy it begs the question, "from where are we drawing our ideas of completeness and effectiveness?"

After having kids, and peeing when sneezing, or not being able to lift things after a c-section, it's understandable that feelings of brokenness can surface.

I (Sarah) remember very soon after the birth of my first child, I actually felt surprised that I was able to breastfeed. For some reason, I had a seed of doubt imbedded in me that wondered if my body would work. I was thrilled when I discovered that it did! I was super stoked! But then fear kicked in when Jackson started favoring one breast. Weeks into breastfeeding, my supply dropped and I started worrying and fretting about my inability to produce milk for our son. Weeks turned into months, and though to everyone else, we had a happy, content, and satiated son, I couldn't shake the feeling that I was lacking. I mean I had to stuff one bra with extra nursing pads because my boobs were so lopsided!! How could I **not** be inadequate?

I (Jenny) remember believing I should be able to carry on my normal role in our home the day we brought Luci home from the hospital. I didn't ask for help, I tried to make us dinner that night and couldn't figure out why the next day my feet had swollen to the size of two watermelons. It didn't take long for me to realize I didn't want to ask Franklin for help. I wanted to show him I could have a baby and keep going like nothing happened. It finally came to a terrible boiling point the night that while sobbing from exhaustion, I picked Luci up and marched out of our bedroom while muttering every expletive you can think of. Franklin gently came into her bedroom and asked if he could help. I was so empty both physically and emotionally I had to say "yes." I walked back to our bedroom feeling like a failure of a mother.

This is not new, ya'll. Women all over, women in all generations, have been feeling this way. And this is exactly why we need each other. This is why we need to reach out and get real and remind each other to give ourselves a break, to give ourselves grace. The idea of completeness or effectiveness isn't one that you can just sling over a woman like a wet blanket. It's not something that you can just wear as a one-size fits all garment. Our beautiful uniqueness, our individuality, our exquisite gifts and abilities are ours and ours alone. Those are the aspects of us, which make us incredibly equipped to handle the ups and downs of motherhood, despite the messages that tell us otherwise.

Last chapter we declared our acceptance of change. The moment we birthed our first baby, we added another layer of responsibility on top of our wide shoulders, and in case you haven't noticed yet, this new job comes with intense emotional and physical demands. We are moms, friends, partners, employees, and volunteers, all of which require us to give away pieces of ourselves. In all of these roles, "normal" tells us that being valuable requires perfection. Friends, that's a heavy load to bear.

Have you ever had a day when you can't stand to be touched by a human being ever again? Rather than feel like a loser mom who's a jerk because she wants space, what if instead we recognized that we are not unlimited resources and more than likely we're just exhausted because we have been giving 100% to our kids?

The truth is we have limited hours in the day. We have limited energy. We have limited physical abilities. It's fact. We have limited resources. No matter how our bodies function after having a baby, the truth is we will ALWAYS have limitations. We're not defective. We're human beings with the same confines every other person experiences.

Needing space, needing a reprieve, needing an adventure, needing time to create, needing to be able to finish a meal while it's still hot, doesn't make us inadequate moms. It makes us…moms. No adjective. No value label. It makes us moms.

Battling fear of inadequacy requires us to be kind to ourselves and embrace grace. **"Normal" tells us that in order to be valuable, we need to be perfect. Grace tells us we are valuable in our imperfection.**

Fear of Vulnerability

I (Jenny) remember super clearly what I ate for dinner the night I had Levi. Beans. Big fat pinto beans with ketchup and sriracha. I remember it because I can vividly recall pooping it out all over the bed while I was pushing. I kept apologizing over and over to Franklin and my midwife while realizing there wasn't much I could do about it. It was one of the most exposed and vulnerable moments of my life.

That moment was impactful because being that vulnerable and dependent on others is scary and uncomfortable. My parents raised me to not depend on anyone else and to always be able to take care of myself. Unfortunately, I took that to the extreme end of the spectrum and experienced years of struggling to be honest about my struggles, ask for help, or share the imperfect places of my life.

However, when we had Levi, I had no choice but to ask for help. In my broken way it sounded something like this, "Hey Mom, so I think I'm feeling a little overwhelmed. But I know you're really busy. If you have any spare time it would be fun to see you."

What I really should've said was, "Mom, I'm dying. I'm not sleeping, I hate my life, I feel hopeless, overwhelmed, and I can't stop crying. I just yelled at the 2-year old and I just want Levi to stop screaming and take a damn nap. Please come help me."

That season of life was still one of the hardest times I've experienced. Sadly, it didn't have to be. I could've been honest and asked for help. Instead, I was afraid to invite others into what felt like chaos.

Since writing this book with Sarah, I've experienced tremendous personal healing, if for no other reason than I've spent 2 years being vulnerable with a friend. She's listened as I've shared my struggles, offering empathy and encouragement. And she's also said, "Jenny, do you really want to write about your poop in our book? Isn't that TMI?" (Sarah note: that was probably my own fear of vulnerability speaking.)

Allowing others to know our struggles allows us to find healing. It's actually extremely cathartic and can help us identify any lies we might believe about our post-partum reality. Fear of being exposed or fully seen and known is a powerful driver. We know several moms who have avoided getting care for post-partum depression because they were afraid to share what they were experiencing.

This fear of vulnerability can also hurt our relationship with our partners. When we can't be honest about what we need it creates anger, resentment, and over time, bitterness.

As we started working on this book and created the body after baby survey, I (Sarah) decided that it would be a good idea for me to take the survey too. One of the last questions is "What does your partner think of your post-partum body?" I left that one blank because honestly I didn't want to ask Steve. I felt embarrassed. And after all we've been through; it struck me as odd that I would feel that way. I was surprised at myself.

One night, some friends offered to watch our kids so we could go out on a date. Our positive and connecting date night turned into a "discussion" about our lack of communication, which turned into an argument. Rather than asking Steve what he thought about my body, I accused him. I said, *"And by the way, I'm supposed to be writing a book on body after kids and we've heard from hundreds of women who seem to know what their partners think of their bodies, and I have no freaking clue what you think about mine because you never tell me."*

Throwing darts is a very effective detour around true vulnerability.

The truth of the situation was that I needed affirmation from Steve but my fear topped with a dollop of pride kept me from asking him for it. I verbally threw up on the poor man because I had stuffed all my insecurities and fears down and let them linger there for way too long. I have since committed myself to growing in this area by opening up and choosing vulnerability more often than not. I'm pretty sure our date nights will be a lot more fun.

Let's all decide to open up. Let's start small, one thing at a time. Take a small step and test it out and see what sweet rewards you see in your relationship with your partner and your friends. Share something that feels a little uncomfortable. Just try it. We believe you'll be met with empathy and encouragement.

94

Feel It

Fear often becomes a backdrop for our lives without us even realizing it. Our environment perpetuates the culture of fear, especially among women, and these things don't just evaporate and disappear. They take root in our minds. They settle in and make a home. They congregate and create our sense of "normal" and the result is a redefined reality. A reality we passively constructed and now live within. All fear isn't bad. (The fear of running in a dark alley at night is pretty legit.) However, fear that causes us to change our lifestyle and becomes consuming is unhealthy.

The first step in conquering this silent stalker sounds, well, crazy. Rather than fight against our fear, we must allow ourselves to feel it however we need. Crying on the floor until you don't have any tears left, screaming at the top of your lungs until you're hoarse, or even punching a bag until you're sweaty and tired are all great ways to face and feel fear.

When we hug it out with anxiety, it loses power. Once we feel it, rather than run from it, we can effectively begin to fight. We do that with perspective.

When we're feeling our fear, thinking about it and reflecting on it, we're able to shift our perception to view our situation differently. It's like turning the bedroom light on after seeing a monster-looking shadow and realizing it's actually just your grandma's ugly lamp.

(Sarah note: grandma is on a roll with her ugly gnome and ugly lamp.)

Most of us know about the great artist Michelangelo's masterpiece sculpture: *David*. At 14 feet high, this 1504 A.D. marble statue beautifully portrays the Biblical hero and is one of the most famous statues in the world[xiv]. It's also a brilliant story of perspective shift.

In 1464 the Opera del Duomo initially commissioned the project and obtained a large block of marble for their first artist. But by 1475 the marble had been rejected by two artists as flawed and unworkable, both fearing the stone had too many imperfections with which to work. The rejected marble sat abandoned in a courtyard for the next 25 years.

Then, in 1501 at the young, tender age of 26, Michelangelo courageously accepted the marble and the challenge of finishing the original commission. He was already one of the highest paid and famous artists and yet he risked his very reputation and took on this disparaged stone. Forget fear of failure. Over the next 2 years he took the imperfect block of marble and created a masterpiece. He had a different perspective from the other artists. Instead of seeing the marble as "flawed" he saw the marble as "valuable" and created a cherished masterpiece from it.

Michelangelo chose to take what others feared and rejected and viewed it differently. He shifted his perspective, shifted the public's perspective, and for hundreds of years the world has been inspired by this incredible work of art. The same block of marble that sat worthlessly abandoned in a courtyard, is now seen as a priceless masterpiece.

And so, like Michelangelo, when we shift our perspective, we shift the result. We chisel away the layers we've built as we've devalued our worth and instead begin to:

→ Shift our perspective from being undesirable to being confident of our gifts and talents and the beauty they bring.

→ Shift our perspective from the idea that perfection gives us worth, to acknowledging all the ways we bring about goodness.

→ Shift our perspective from fearing honesty to realizing others just might find their own personal freedom hearing our struggles. (They also might really enjoy caring for you in the midst of them.)

Nelson Mandela, former President of South Africa said, *"I learned that courage was not the absence of fear, but the triumph over it. The brave man is not he who does not feel afraid, but he who conquers that fear."*xv

We don't measure our contentment or our courage by the absence of fear. Instead, it's what we do with the fear that is an indicator of our growth. "Normal" runs and hides, self-medicates, or ignores. Courageous contentment stares it down, tears it down, and rebuilds it with indestructible truth.

May we all be moms of indestructible truth and unbreakable peace.

Recap

✓ Fear is our biggest contributor to our discontentment.

✓ Three of the main fears that many of us face are:
   The fear of being undesirable.
   The fear of inadequacy.
   The fear of vulnerability.

✓ We have tools to overcome fear.
   1. We can choose truth.
   2. We can open up and get honest.
   3. We can feel it and face it.

✓ A perspective shift means we shift the result.

Action Steps
Journal or Discuss

- What fears do you have about:
    - Being undesirable?
    - Being inadequate?
    - Being honest/vulnerable?

- What are some choices you can make to help you say yes to freedom from fear?

- What are some things your partner could do to help in this fight?

- Once you've identified them, be brave and share them with your partner—be vulnerable, and be prepared for them to respond imperfectly. Share what you need from them and give them grace and give grace to yourself too.

6

Connecting with Our Partners

He says I'm beautiful and all that stuff but I don't believe him.

HEATHER, mom of 2

Marjorie William's classic children's novel, *The Velveteen Rabbit,* tells the story of a stuffed toy rabbit given to a young boy for Christmas. The velveteen rabbit spends his days in the playroom with a myriad of the other toys, longing for the day when the young boy will play with him.

Eventually, the timid rabbit befriends the tattered Skin Horse, who, as the wisest toy of the playroom, divulges that the goal of all nursery toys is to ultimately be made "real" through the love of a human. Their conversation one evening goes like this:

"What is REAL?' asked the Rabbit one day, as they were lying side by side near the nursery fender, just before Nana came in to tidy up the room. 'Does it mean having things that buzz inside you and a stick-out handle?'

'Real isn't how you are made,' said the Skin Horse. 'It's a thing that happens to you. When a child loves you for a long, long time, not just to play with, but REALLY loves you, then you become Real.'

'Does it hurt?' asked the Rabbit.
'Sometimes,' said the Skin Horse, for he was always truthful. 'When you are Real, you don't mind being hurt.'

'Does it happen all at once, like being wound up,' he asked, 'or bit by bit?'

'It doesn't happen all at once,' said the Skin Horse. 'You become. It takes a long time. That's why it doesn't often happen to people who break easily, or have sharp edges, or who have to be carefully kept. Generally, by the time you are Real, most of your hair has been loved off; and your eyes drop out and you get loose in the joints and very shabby. But these things don't matter at all, because once you are Real, you can't be ugly except to people who don't understand.'"

As I (Sarah) celebrate my 15th wedding anniversary this year, I can say with certainty this incredibly insightful and beautiful depiction of relationships is right on. Realness happens in our lives when we give ourselves fully to those who love us. It comes at a cost to us. We avail ourselves to a complete emptying out in our marriages, and in our resulting motherhood. What we gain in all of this is pretty incredible—at the end of the pouring out, we are seen and known by people who understand us—if we let them.

This isn't a marriage book. But we are delving into our partner dynamic because we believe there's incredible strength, support, and connection that resides there and we need to tap into it as we walk this contentment road.

Sadly, our "normal" for relationships after having a baby is pretty abysmal. In a 2-year study of over 2,000 parents, researchers found, [xvi]

> *"About 30% remained at about the same state of happiness or better once they had the baby, according to self-reported measures of well-being. The rest said their happiness decreased during the first and second year after the birth."*

Another study found[xvii],

> *"Compared with pre-birth levels and trajectories, parents showed sudden deterioration following birth on observed and self-reported measures of positive and negative aspects of relationship functioning. The deterioration in these variables was small to medium in size and tended to persist throughout the remaining years of the study."*

Fortunately, we believe it doesn't have to be this way. Statistics can be changed. And like the Velveteen Rabbit, we can experience true love and connection with our partners when we get Real.

Coach Barbara

It was 2007 and Steve and I (Sarah) found ourselves in Barbara's office, a marriage counselor. Sitting there on opposite sides of the couch, Barbara behind her desk, we were finally admitting to ourselves, and to a complete stranger, we needed some marriage coaching.

We had been married for 5 years. Basically, we were toddlers in our marriage relationship and yet, here we were, facing new marital territory that required skills we'd never been trained in. That's where coach Barbara came along.

Looking back on that season of marital growth, it's pretty easy to see where we'd drifted apart. The first 3 years of our marriage, Steve was home only half of the time, the rest was spent on deployment or detachments or other training with the Navy. Yes, it was tough. Spending our first wedding anniversary and second and third away from each other wasn't what I imagined, but despite the distance, we adapted.

While he was gone we worked hard at connecting. Facetime and Skype weren't around yet and so we decided to journal. We each had a journal and would write to each other whenever we could. Once every month or so, we would send each other our journals.

This was such an important way for us to connect despite the miles. We shared our deepest thoughts and longings—things that we wouldn't bother to share during a short phone call. It was intentional, vulnerable, and effective. Once he returned home, the fire we worked so hard to keep aflame was still going strong.

But then we changed duty stations and Steve began his "shore tour," keeping him home for 3 years. Surprisingly, or maybe not, we entered a time in our marriage when things got complacent. We took each other for granted and started drifting. The independence that served us so well while we were apart, started to divide us.

That season of my life was not only incredibly lonely, but also joyless. When we stopped doing the little things required for us to emotionally connect, we also stopped physically connecting. With the absence of both forms of intimacy, I felt lost. Both Steve and I needed to reestablish the intentional rhythms that helped us enjoy one another. Moving back towards deeper intimacy moved me back to feeling at peace with our marriage.

Connecting with someone communicates we have worth to that person. It bestows on us value and significance. When we feel valuable to our partners, we experience relational peace. When we experience relational peace, we're much more willing to offer up more of ourselves for connection. The more we connect with our partners, the more peace we experience, which can ultimately translate into a foundation of contentment.

Laying the Foundation

One of the beautiful aspects about being a woman is our ability to powerfully feel. It can also be the area in our lives that gets overlooked the most and given the least credit. Emotions are multi-dimensional and can often add layers of complexity to our relationships. These ever-changing dynamics force us to relentlessly work at understanding and managing them. And because "normal" sells us on-demand living, our threshold for patiently working at anything is getting lower. Connecting with our partner on a meaningful heart level takes time. And while "normal" sells us passion-driven sex, if we don't establish a real and deep connection, we risk laying a foundation that crumbles at the first sign of difficulty. Which is what often can happen after having a baby.

And so, our goal becomes finding and investing in a healthy balance of emotional and physical connection with our partners. When this happens, we lay the groundwork for experiencing deeper contentment.

So how exactly do we emotionally connect with our partners? The keys are time, talk, and touch.

Time

As moms, time is a valuable commodity in our lives. Most often we're the hub that keeps the wheel grinding in our families and sometimes at a cost to ourselves. I

THE WAR ON NORMAL

(Jenny) have been in a desperate need of a haircut for a few months. I scheduled an appointment last week and had to cancel it because a meeting ran over. I was so frustrated that Franklin offered to cut my hair for me. How kind. And ridiculous.

When we pour resources into something, we assign them value. For example, when we make saving for retirement a priority and allocate our income to do that, we're saying retirement savings is a priority and worth our resources. When we forgo a new pair of shoes so our kid can take an art class, we're assigning a higher value to fostering their creativity than we are on shoes. Every decision we make assigns either greater or lesser value.

Time is a resource and the way we use it assigns greater or lesser value to our partner. If we're not leveraging our time and investing it in our relationship, then we'll see diminishing returns. This works the same way with friendships. (Which we'll talk about in a few chapters!)

In economics, there's a principle known as the law of diminishing returns. It tells us when we add something new into a process, without taking something away, over time, we'll see our return get smaller. It's no different with our investment of time. When we add to our schedules, without taking away from our schedules, something will suffer. Something's gotta give.

We can't let our relationship with our partner experience diminishing returns or it will affect how emotionally connected we are and whether or not our relationship survives at all. And this will absolutely decrease our output of contentment.

We get to put the time in. We don't have to. We can choose to drift apart and experience deeper and deeper discontentment. We *get* to put the time into connecting with our partner, which is both a great responsibility and a great privilege. And it doesn't just require time. It also requires us to share ourselves through talk.

Talk

There are many days as mothers when we simply can't say another word. The constant questions, "Why mommy?" as our curious learners are striving to understand the world around them, are exhausting to navigate. My (Sarah's) friend told me recently that at the end of the day *"I had used up all my words."* The tank was empty. The well was dry. Once the kids were in bed, it was time to clock out, tap out. I'm pretty sure the phrase *"Netflix and chill"* was coined by an exhausted mom.

If you have a partner, chances are, meaningful conversation doesn't happen during this time. Before you know it, days go by and the stories you wanted to share about what happened in your day become faint memories and don't seem so important. Over time, there are parts of your life your partner might not even know about, not for lack of caring, rather lack of you sharing.

Throughout our day we talk to everyone *but* our partner and suddenly there's a wall that, over time, can turn into an entire fortress. Suddenly, we're living a disconnected

THE WAR ON NORMAL

life. We stop sharing our entire life with our spouse and instead, share it with someone else. This is how marriages end.

As busy women, partners, and mothers, it's crucial that we leave some gas in the tank and some water in the well for our spouses. And the same goes for them too. It needs to be mutual for it to work. As we venture further into our marriages, it's not a no-brainer. Because, let's be honest: it requires something of us; an investment. It takes effort. It takes committing to asking your partner how their day was and sharing how yours went. It also requires one on one time when you are dreaming together, laughing together, crying together, and hoping together. Sharing ourselves by sharing the most mundane parts of our days to the most outlandish dreams we have, are crucial parts of establishing peace in our partnerships. The more at peace we feel, the more we'll welcome the physical expression of connectedness...SEX.

Touch (physical connection)

Statistically speaking, talking comes easier to women than to men (we know there are exceptions to this generalization, those with husbands who love to talk.) While talking is a way many of us enjoy connecting with our partners, we believe that sex isn't only a powerful connector, it's also a NECESSARY one.

I (Sarah) clearly remember sitting in my doctor's office for my 6-week check-up after baby. She gave me the double thumbs up to resume, what I affectionately call, "sexercise." Let's just say, that leaving her office that day, I was not running down the hall clicking my heels in glee. I kinda looked at her all crazy like "sex...what??" Who in the world is actually thinking about s-e-x right now? (Besides every post-partum hubby on the face of the earth who is in need of some action.)

Just because we get the "all clear" from our provider, does not mean that we are necessarily ready physically, emotionally, or mentally, to get back into the saddle. Cowgirls need some time to get ready to giddy-up. (Jenny side note: apologies for Sarah's northern attempts at referencing cowgirls.)

Vicki, mom of one, shared with us how she reconnected with her husband after she gave birth. She asked herself, *"what does it look like for me to give myself fully to my hubs?"* That question was the driving force behind the small steps they took towards their goal of sex after she was healing from a C-section. The first step for Vicki was to simply feel comfortable and content being naked in front of her spouse.

> *"I was prepared for this [sex] to be a struggle. Hubby and I talked a lot about how it might be different and ways we can react and talk through it. Before returning to sex, we did small things like shower together and did lots of cuddling. I got used to him seeing and touching me naked. I think this made a big difference for us when sex was on the table again.*
>
> *My husband was tender and patient with me. He didn't rush it at all. And, it felt surprisingly good at first and*

now feels better than ever.

*The biggest difference in this area is how I feel about
sex. Sex now feels deeply intimate and incredibly
vulnerable. Pre-baby there was a transactional nature in
it for us and mostly we liked how it felt physically. Now,
it is the most vulnerable thing about our marriage, and it
is the sweetest. It feels like unity and connection."*

What *does* it look like to give ourselves fully to our
partner? What a great question. The answer to this is that
it looks differently for everyone because we are all
unique and at varying places in our relationships with our
bodies and our partners. When we balance time and talk,
touch will come naturally. But let's be real. There are
plenty of date nights when the conversation is perfect
and the time to get out is spot on, but when you come
home, the last thing you want to do is have sex. Most
likely you wanna get your stretchy pants on and get to
bed. Good news, it's okay to occasionally choose that.
It's also important to choose sex when you can. Our
connection can get lopsided if we're not balancing time,
talk and touch.

As we seek to connect physically in our ever-changing
bodies, let's check out 3 dynamics that impact our
physical intimacy with our partner.

1. Self-Care is the new priority.

Making lunches, feeding the baby, managing childcare,
staying on top of laundry, not letting your work team

down, and extracurricular activities will always have a place on your resume. This leaves little room for shaving, bathing, or brushing your teeth, let alone reading your favorite book.

And this isn't just when we bring our baby home. It's as long as they live under our roof. No matter what stage our kids are in, we'll always have a tendency to prioritize everyone and everything over our own needs. Sex and reconnection with our partner easily fall to the end of the list, especially if we're not taking care of ourselves.

Self-care requires answering some tough questions. Like, what do I need? What brings me fulfillment? What makes me feel re-charged? What do I crave? Quiet time? Time with friends? Adventure? And then, how do I even ask for this? Sometimes the most challenging part about this need for a fill 'er up moment, is asking for it. Because how in the world do we ask for something that perhaps we've never needed before?

Most often as we start thinking of these things and even asking for them guilt will, at some point, begin to creep in. It accuses us with thoughts of selfishness or inadequacy or being a bad mom. And it's a lie. The most selfless thing we can do as moms is make sure we're full enough to care for our families.

Steve and I (Sarah) were married 7 years before we started our family. I remember feeling absolutely run down and run out and run over after giving birth. I had the runs. I just couldn't bring myself to ask Steve for what I needed. I felt like after all this time, he should be able to read my mind; even though I couldn't even read my own mind...those damn hormones were in the way.

Poor hubs, I was basically asking him to put a puzzle together while blindfolded and handcuffed with earplugs in. The man could do no right. It was miserable for both of us. The issue at hand was communication. I couldn't bring myself to ask him for what I needed. Pride was standing in my way. (Remember the fear of being vulnerable?)

Finally I got to a breaking point a few months after Jackson was born. We were so disconnected and miserable. I told him that I needed him to take over and take charge. I told him that even though I felt anxious about it, I needed to have a date night with him. So we got a babysitter to come over and we went to listen to some live music three minutes from our house. Sitting there listening to this flamenco guitarist, I was gripping my phone like it was my lifeline. I was so anxious. I couldn't fully be present with Steve, even though I knew I needed and wanted to be. Our sitter texted and said Jackson was upset and wouldn't settle down and go to sleep. I was about to jet out of there so fast. Steve put his hand on my arm and said, *"He will be okay. He's safe. He's loved. He's been fed. He's okay."* So we stayed 30 more minutes and then came home in a blaze of glory.

Years later, we still look back on that night and chuckle. I was literally on the edge of my seat ready to bolt at any second, the entire 1.5 hours we were gone. I remember so clearly the anxiety I felt about being away while also feeling conflicted because I knew we needed it. Steve and I needed to reconnect.

It definitely didn't happen that night, bless Steve's heart—even though he did exactly what I needed and wanted him to do. But it was the beginning of my journey towards accepting the fact that I needed to ask for Steve to help me refill my tank when I was getting low. As an introvert, often, that meant simply going to the grocery store alone or going on a walk alone, or getting everyone to clear out of the house so I can have alone time at home. This is self-care—prioritizing our needs over the needs of our families.

Airlines know all about this idea of self-care. Put your oxygen mask on first, before you put on the kid's mask. You can't help anyone when you're gasping for air.

2. Hormones: the new third wheel.

I (Jenny) used to believe my will was stronger than my hormones. I believed that I could control my emotions enough to rein in any influence hormones might have over my life. I thought I was doing a really great job until I had kids and found myself crying on the toilet, devastated by constipation. It was then I realized that hormones would always have a place in my life, in my marriage (and in my bowel habits).

Did you know that the biggest drop in hormone levels that we will ever experience in our lives happens after we give birth? Those hormones continue to impact us months after giving birth and as we age. They will never go away but will always change in their impact on us. Our connection with our partners is helped when we understand the role hormones can play in how we feel and think about our bodies and life in general.

Body awareness—specifically, recognizing what and how hormones affect our bodies—is an important dynamic in connecting with our partners. This helps to foster open and honest communication.

The same hormones that ushered us into puberty also helped our bodies prepare for pregnancy, to safely carry and grow a baby, and then actually helped us become mothers after we gave birth. These same hormones, which introduced us to motherhood, also usher us into menopause where tampons go to hell and are replaced with hot flashes....from hell.

One common hormone you've probably heard of is oxytocin. It's incredible really. "*Oxytocin actually alters our brain and probably permanently changes our brain by 'turning on' the areas we need for mothering,*" says Dr. Sarah Buckley, MD and expert on hormones. After we give birth we have an incredible surge in oxytocin, the biggest surge we'll ever experience in our entire lives. The oxytocin chemically bonds us to our babies. Dads get this influx too, but it's not quite as strong as ours.

You've heard of those moms who have super human strength when their baby is in danger. They'll pick up a car or jump through a burning house to save their baby. Our brains get flooded with these natural chemicals (hormones), which fuel our muscles with these bursts of super human strength or courage. It's really incredible how we're created to nurture and protect our babies.

And oxytocin is only one of many hormones that course through our bodies, each with unique jobs to do. Our estrogen levels drop after we give birth, which prevent us from ovulating (thank you baby Jesus) but also lower our sex drive and cause us to be a bit dry down south.

Hormones impact our bodies physically and emotionally. This complicates how we connect with our partner. If we're feeling particularly bloated and breaking out, most likely we're not gonna feel super desirable. This impacts our partner, who might just have sex on the brain. So then we say no, they get their feelings hurt, then we get into a fight and we cry 'cause our feelings are now hurt and we feel ugly, so we (and our hormones) go sleep on the couch. Alone.

Hormones are a factor in our ability to physically and emotionally reconnect with our spouse. If we ignore them we set ourselves up for shame and disappointment. When we learn to recognize their influence and manage our response to them, it can bring peace and contentment with our current reality.

When I (Sarah) am aware of how my hormones work and affect my feelings and thoughts, I can share them with Steve and we can adjust our expectations of how we connect. For me, I keep up with my cycle on an app—yes, there is an app for that. This alerts me to the weeks when I might be feeling particularly emotional—and this isn't an excuse for bad behavior. I tell Steve, *"I'm pmsing this week and feeling super cranky. Can you please give me some extra love and support?"* Being self-aware and willing to share with our partners, sets us up for an opportunity to grow in our teamwork. Whereas, ignoring our hormones creates confusion and unnecessary turmoil in our relationships.

And just to close this conversation out, we also want to add that post-birth blues happen for many, if not most mamas. That big hormone drop is to blame for that. But if you're feeling that you're not bonding with your baby, or catch yourself thinking thoughts about yourself or your baby that are harmful in nature—please tell your spouse, your best friend, and especially your doctor or midwife. This is that moment when you need to ask for an extra hand, to make an appointment to see your provider and let them know what's going on. Post-partum depression is real and it can be incredibly destructive to you, your baby, and your partner. Very often it's something that medication or other alternatives can really help with. You're not alone. You're not unique in this struggle. You have what it takes to step out and connect with others who love and can help you.

3. Going from Mama Bear to Sexy Mama.

"It's quite strange for my boobs to be used in a sexual manner since for the past 6.5 months my baby girl has been sucking on them for nourishment practically non-stop. It almost feels weird when my husband touches them. It's almost like I want to say, "No, these are Sophia's right now." Ashley, mom of 1.

In the midst of adjusting to our new reality in virtually every other facet of our lives and bodies, we now realize that seeing ourselves as sexual beings feels kinda strange! And then, when we think that it's strange, that we think it's strange; it trips us up even more. Ya know?

Our (Sarah's) kiddos slept in our room in a co-sleeper for the first six months. And even though they were itty-bitty babies, I felt kinda dirty having sex in the bed right next to them! I felt even worse if we put them in the adjacent bathroom or anywhere else other than where we were. It felt like a no win. I kinda wanted them to wear earmuffs. It was awkward.

Then there was the unease I felt about my body…the flop…the squish…the disconcerting feeling that we were about to get surprised at any moment by something we weren't expecting. I was terrified and so tense. I think Steve was oblivious to it all and was just super thankful that I had surrendered myself to him, well, my body, my mind was not in the moment…at all.

Apparently, Rachael, mom of 1, has the same challenge, *"Mentally getting to a place where I want to be sexual takes a lot more effort. It's difficult turning off 'mommy brain.'"*

How in the world do we go from a full-time mama bear to a sexy mama?

I mentioned earlier that Steve and I (Sarah) had been married for 7 years before having kids. And I am horrified to admit that as I was trying to solve this mama bear to lover situation, I decided to go through my lingerie drawer. This was probably about one year after Jackson was born. I decided that I needed to dress the part. That in order to really feel sexy, I should probably start with wearing something other than sweats. So I busted out these black lace boy short looking underwear and thought triumphantly, *"this'll do it."*

Moments later, I looked down and noticed black lace molting all over my body. Ladies, my lingerie was so old that it was disintegrating on my nether-regions; black lace shards were all over the place! I was laughing while horrified. I immediately changed back into my sweats, and went online and ordered some new stuff. And guys, for me, this was the ticket to helping me feel 1. Excited about sex, and 2. Like a lover again. New lingerie was the key for me. It might not be for you, in fact, it's not for Jenny. Our goal is to find what it is that helps us personally get to a relaxed and excited place.

Another recent discovery for me (Sarah) is flirting with my husband throughout the day. Just recently, Steve left me a love note inside the fridge. Without going too much into detail (and giving away his secret sauce), Steve wrote some cute, but funny love type things. He probably didn't realize this at the time, but what he was actually doing was turning on what I like to call "the crotchpot." It took all day, dammit, but by the time he got home that night, *Ding Ding*, I was hot and ready. For you, it could simply be taking a shower, a bath, or having a few moments of alone time to switch gears. But allow yourself some time to transition mentally so that you can turn on physically.

No matter what age our kids are, being sexual is part of our being. When we ignore that aspect of who we are and only try to turn it on in the bedroom, it can create a mental tension (and stage fright!). When Steve and I show each other affection throughout the day it helps the kids see healthy connection and helps me acknowledge that aspect of my being.

Believe Them

Stop and take a deep breath and reflect on how you're currently feeling. After reading about connecting to your partner, what's your primary feeling? Hope? Anger? Frustration? Longing? Joy?

Thinking through how we connect can bring up a spectrum of emotions that, even if painful, can lead us to opportunities for personal growth. In this moment of reflection, it's important to point out that none of these ways of connecting will produce long-lasting contentment if they're not built on the foundation of trust. While we work on intimacy we must also work on believing on our partners.

The Jewish apostle Paul said in one of his documented letters[xviii], "*Whatever is true, whatever is noble, whatever is right, whatever is pure, whatever is lovely, whatever is admirable—if anything is excellent or praiseworthy—think about such things.*"

Those are lofty goals compared to what we typically think of our post-baby bodies. Most often our heads are not filled with super true, lovely, or excellent thoughts about ourselves. However, if we asked our partners their thoughts, we believe we'd get a different story. They see us as so much more than our post-baby bodies. They see our intelligence, our humor, our kindness, our strength, our ability to birth and care for a tiny human. They see Super Woman even if we see Granny Smith. They experience us in the totality of ourselves rather than a mere body.

"I have a wonderful husband who thinks I'm still as sexy as the day we met. Part of me thinks he needs a CAT scan, but I see him that same way too. So in this area I ease up as they are his feelings about me, not mine thankfully!" Rachael, mom of 3.

"He says I'm beautiful, but I'm sure he'd like my previous body better." Sonya, mom of 1.

"He claims to love it…but I think he just wants sex!" Sarah, mom of 2.

"I think he is a bit disgusted with it. That might be too strong a word but I think he misses tight and toned. And I think he is annoyed by my lack of motivation to fix it right now." Christy, mom of 2.

"He loves me and tells me I'm beautiful. However I know when we have sex he sometimes isn't sure where to grab on because it's so squishy…" Jen, mom of 6.

Can you relate to any of those sentiments? We can. With the birth of a child we also birth the tension between how we see ourselves versus how our partners view our bodies. When it comes to seeing what they see, it can be easy to brush off their compliments and observations. Often we think they have an ulterior motive or need to have their head examined. Fueling contentment can only happen in our relationships when we chose to believe what our partners tell us about how they see our bodies.

"He loves me no matter how I look. He loves sex with me and makes me feel sexy. But I have to allow myself to believe that as well—and trust that it's true. It makes our sex hotter and better." Sarah, mom of 2.

"My husband is either the best liar in the world, or he genuinely loves my body. He even loves my body when I'm pregnant. But when he loves my body the most is when I love it." Laura, mom of 5.

You may not see yourself that way and that's okay for now. Trust that what they're telling you *is* true. Trust awakens confidence in us and gives us the freedom and space to grow. It also lays the foundation for connection. We can't fully give ourselves to someone we don't believe.

Recap

Phew. We've covered a lot in this chapter.

- ✓ There are two main forms of connectedness, physical and emotional.
- ✓ When we're connected on both levels, our body contentment is higher.
- ✓ Emotional connectedness requires time and talk, and leads to the physical connection of touch.
- ✓ There are 3 dynamics that impact our physical intimacy that keep us from reconnecting
  - Self-Care
- ✓ Hormones: the new third wheel.
- ✓ Embracing our sexual-self and our nurturing-self.

- ✓ We choose to believe the truths our partners see in us and say to us.
- ✓ Trust is the foundation of connectedness.

Action Steps
Journal or Discuss

The point of this chapter is to help us be intentional about connecting with our partner in hopes of experiencing deeper contentment with ourselves. This can be risky or can be exciting depending on where you are with a partner.

Some of the suggestions we give may work for you while others might be better implemented at a later time or just chucked altogether. Just promise us you'll try some of them. Take a risk. Be brave. Connectedness with our partners is worth it.

✖ **Time-** Plan a date night that requires you to create together. Take cooking classes, paint something, plant something. Pick anything that requires you to work together to create. Don't make it complicated. Make it fun and simple.

✖ **Talk-** Find space to listen and be heard with your partner. Grab a fun drink or snack and spend time asking the following questions.

1. What are you learning about yourself?
2. What do you appreciate about me?
3. What do you want to do together this year?
4. What is one of your goals or dreams?
5. How are you different from when we first got together?
6. What do you love about us?
7. What would you like to do more of together?

✖ **Touch-** Flirt up a storm with your significant other. Revert back to your 18-year-old self if necessary. Think about what makes them feel desired and valued and pursue them that way. Start in the morning and see where it leads. Be intentional. Write a note if that helps. Have fun with it and enjoy the response.

THE WAR ON NORMAL

7

Arming Our Kids for Battle

I have come to the conclusion that I need to be more gentle with myself. Maybe because I now have a daughter and realize how vital my role is in shaping her sense of self.

SARAH, mom of 2

One night Franklin and Luci were spending some quality time together while I (Jenny) took a shower. Franklin was cleaning out the dishwasher while Luci watched. He pulled out a few water bottle tops and set them on the counter as he asked Luci questions about her day. They ended up on the topic of what Luci would do if she were ever to get lost in a crowd and Franklin asked her how she would describe her mom to someone. Without missing a beat, Luci said, *"She looks like an angel in the sky. She has long dark hair...and big nipples." "What?"* Franklin

125

responded, to which Luci pointed to the water bottle tops and said, *"Like these big nipples."*

Kids don't miss much, and the powerful truth is, we are the biggest influence on our kid's body image. How we view and speak about our bodies directly impacts how kids will view and speak about their bodies as they grow.

And we say kids because this isn't just a lesson for our daughters, it's for our sons as well. They're the men who'll be future boyfriends, husbands, partners, and consumers. We can influence all those things for the good if we leverage our guidance wisely.

There are tons of responsibilities we have as parents (just keeping our kids alive is a win some days). Helping our kids be content with their bodies and value the bodies of others is a calling we can't ignore. Understanding how we influence our kids in this battle can be complicated, and in thinking about it, we found ourselves asking the following questions:

1. At what point do kids begin to ascribe value statements to things in life and when do they begin to develop the tendency towards placing good and bad judgments on stuff? (At what age do kids think a woman is more beautiful if she has long hair? Or believe that dresses make a girl pretty?)

2. What's the critical age when kids go down a path of valuing women's bodies or down the path of unhealthy perceptions? (When do girls begin to look at their bodies and call them good or bad *and* alter their behavior accordingly?)

3. And then how do we use this info to help us encourage our kids to value their bodies? (How the heck do we not screw them up?)

Answering, or attempting to answer these important questions, led us to do a little research and soul searching of our own.

What Do You Believe?

In order to help our kids learn how to embrace bodies (yes, bodies of all shapes, sizes, and colors) we spent some time thinking through what we believe about our kids' development and capabilities. We also looked at Freud, Skinner, Piaget, and many other childhood development scholars in an attempt to help us understand how best to influence our kids. (Sarah Note: Jenny attacked the childhood development research like Chuck Norris in a scuffle. She brought it.)

As we compiled countless philosophies, we concluded 4 things about our kids:

1. We believe kids create mental folders called "schemas" that help them interpret and store information. These schemas act like different colored lenses each child wears and the interpretation they make of their surroundings depends on the lenses they're wearing.

   For example if we undress in front of them and grab our stomachs while making a displeasing comment (or noise…insert groan,) then our kids will believe a stomach that looks like the one we're lamenting over, is bad.

2. We believe kids generally start out loving their bodies and loving other people's bodies and are **taught to behave and believe differently**. We think it's our role and privilege to be the protectors and cultivators of the positive schema kids begin with.

3. We believe a kid's culture, their caregivers, parents and friends influence them. We think kids are born with a basic tendency towards learning and their culture teaches them how to successfully function within their cultural norms.

4. We also believe once established, these schemas are extremely difficult to re-wire and we believe we can be the most powerful influencers in our kids' lives. Booyah!

These four beliefs guided us as we answered our questions and asked even bigger ones.

The Big Question

My (Jenny's) Levi is amazing. He's like Indiana Jones and Godzilla wrapped into a monkey. Because of his energy and exuberance for life, I find myself having conversations with my parents that include things like, *"Dad, I'm not sure he's capable of sitting still that long."* Or, *"Mom, I'm not sure he understands what a whisper means."* I have to take into account where he is developmentally, to assess how I teach and guide him.

This becomes the big question: When do kids learn, remember, and build upon the values they're taught?

To get a basic grasp on this from an age and stage perspective, we thought we'd take a look at Jean Piaget's stages of development. (He was the one who coined the word "schema.") Then we'll go to the practical side of all this. (Sarah is starting to hyperventilate from all the serious, research-based talk.)

Piaget believed we could loosely classify kids into the following developmental stages:

Sensorimotor (birth to 2 years)	Preoperational (2-7 years)
Baby learns by coordinating sensory experiences with actions. Super big into exploring through the senses like taste, touch, sound, and sight (and all the mamas said "Duh.")	Kids begin to understand symbolic thinking, using words to represent objects, they begin to pretend and are super self-focused and can only see the world from their standpoint. This is where they begin to construct schemas. They begin to understand value systems from a knowledge standpoint but not emotionally.
Concrete Operational (7-11 years)	**Formal Operational (11-15 years)**
Kids can begin to reason logically. This is when judgments begin to take place. Kids are now able to categorize information into different belief sets such as "good" and "bad." They form the categories from 2-7 years and then begin labeling their environment from 7-11. Wow!	Can reason in abstract and logical ways. This is when our kids begin to dream and also form idealistic thoughts. They're still pretty egocentric (self-centered) and think about the world and how it affects them rather than others. They take their constructed beliefs and project them on the world and others, then use their created labels to judge outcomes.

How's This Helpful?

If we know that from the ages of 2-7ish, our kids are creating the folders they'll use to organize their world for the rest of their lives, we can be intentional about the folders we believe are priorities. If being content with their body is a priority we want to instill in our kids, then we'll spend a lot of time helping shape this folder. If we want our kids to value people of all shapes, sizes, and color, we'll put our resources towards forming that folder in our kids. Then we know (or at least hope and freakin' pray) when they hit 7ish-11ish, and as they begin to assign meaning to their world, they'll have healthy folders to use to organize it all.

One Christmas, when Luci was three, I (Jenny) took her to volunteer at a Christmas program. Our job was to pass out cookies to those who came, which of course, was a terrible job for a 3-year-old. You try telling your toddler to not eat the hundreds of cookies in front of her. Geesh.

As we were passing them out, a woman caught Luci's attention as she came through our line. Luci, my curious and outspoken child, yelled out, *"Mommy, why is her bootie soo big?"* At first I tried to shove a cookie in her mouth to shut her up. But she's persistent. *"Mommy* (chew, chew, chew) *why is her bootie so big?"*

JENNY BAKER & SARAH BLIGHT

So I answered her the only way I could even think at that time, *"Because God made her perfectly that way. Isn't she beautiful?"*

Talk about a tough moment. I wasn't prepared to hit that one and I wasn't prepared to see my 3-year-old daughter already noticing body type differences. I could've told her that observation wasn't kind. But, that would've been assigning a negative value. The logic goes something like this:

-*"Don't say things like that. It's not kind."*
-*"Why wasn't it kind?"*
-*" Because it would make the woman feel bad."*
-*"Why would it make her feel bad?"*
-*" Because she has a big bootie and probably feels bad about it."*
-*"Why would she feel bad about a big bootie unless big booties are bad?"*

Or

-*"We shouldn't talk about people out loud."*
 -*"Why not?"*
-*"Because we could hurt someone's feelings."*
-*"Why would a big bootie hurt someone's feelings unless having a big bootie is bad?"*

See? It's freakin' hard. We can inadvertently help our kids create negative body schemas.

Kids pay attention and those observations are healthy and developmentally appropriate which gives us many opportunities to shape what folder they go in! From our

132

personal experience, there are 4 ways we've found to help our kids create positive body image schemas.

1. Celebrate A Growth Mindset

Eating disorders, plastic surgery stats, and consumer spending on beauty products and clothes are skyrocketing because our kids are given the idea or picture
of perfection and will only stop once they believe they've reached it. Anything less is believed to be failure.

And so, our job just got a whole lot more challenging. We now need to thoughtfully teach our kids how to appreciate where they are, while also not being afraid to work towards where they want to be. Remember in Chapter 3 when we said "growth is measured by movement?" It's growth that we want to focus on with our kids, the effort, the hard work and the persistence it takes not to give up and throw in the towel. Any forward movement is growth and that is what we celebrate.

There's a woman by the name of Carol Dweck, a psychology professor at Stanford University, who has been a researcher in the field of motivation and how to foster success.

> "My research shows that praise for intelligence or ability backfires. What we've shown is that when you praise someone, say, 'You're smart at this,' the next time they struggle, they think they're not. It's really about praising the process they engage in, not how smart they are or how good they are at it, but taking on

difficulty, trying many different strategies, sticking to it, and achieving over time."[xix]

Salman Khan, founder of the Khan Academy, seems to take this similar approach with his kids when he shared this in an op-ed for the *Huffington Post*:[xx]

> *"My 5-year—old son has just started reading. Every night, we lay on his bed and he reads a short book to me. Inevitably, he'll hit a word that he has trouble with: last night the word was "gratefully." He eventually got it after a fairly painful minute. He then said, "Dad, aren't you glad how I struggled with that word? I think I could feel my brain growing."*

Khan explained that based on research he *"decided to praise my son not when he succeeded at things he was already good at, but when he persevered with things that he found difficult. I stressed to him that by struggling, your brain grows."* It's called a growth mindset.

Why is this important to include in a chapter about teaching our kids how to create positive body schemas? Because our bodies are constantly changing!!! Men go bald, we go gray, things don't stay in the same place. Contentment says, *"I'm okay with how things are, sometimes there are things I can do to change the things I don't like, but my value doesn't change when my body does."* But there are times when even hard work doesn't get us there. I (Sarah) have mentioned I have zero boobs. No matter how much I "work" at getting bigger boobs it's not gonna happen. This is obviously an area I can't change with work and because my value isn't wrapped up in an "end" result I'm (learning) to be okay with it. Seriously, it's a daily struggle.

When our kids have a growth mindset, they're not wrecked when things get hard and require work. They don't feel like failures, rather they feel secure in their value, separate from a result.

If we only focus on being smart, or beautiful, or clever, or reaching a number, we are setting our kids up for a lifetime of bitter disappointment. What happens if they're in college and they gain the freshman 15? They don't see the beauty anymore; they are focused on the number. What happens when our daughters or daughters-in-law have had babies and they don't look the same as they used to? They must not be desirable. When we drill down and get specific with our kids (and that's the key, getting specific) and really dial them into the attributes that underpin the beauty and wit and intelligence and health, then we're really onto something meaningful and helpful for them as they become adults. When we exemplify what it looks like to value the process more than the results, our kids learn to appreciate and celebrate growth.

One last thing to add to this dialogue about the growth mindset—working on these things with our kids helps us to be mindful of our own personal growth. We slow down, we think before we speak (or before we groan) or before we communicate to our kids. Ya'll, this is to our benefit. It gives us a chance to grow *with* our kids. It's a healing work that is important in our lives just as much as it is for theirs.

2. Redefine Beauty

Pause for a moment and define beauty. We really mean it. Stop and give it some thought. How would you define it with words? What does it visually look like? Where do you most often see it? Is it something that can be felt?

Dove, the soap people, released a report in 2011 called "*The Real Truth About Beauty: Revisited.*" The study revealed that only 4% of women around the world consider themselves beautiful, and that anxiety about looks begins at an early age.

According to Dove's investigation of over 1,200 10-to-17-year-olds, 72%, said they felt tremendous pressure to be beautiful. The study also found that only 11% of girls around the world feel comfortable using the word beautiful to describe their looks, showing that there is a universal increase in beauty pressure and a decrease in girls' confidence as they grow older.[xxi]

"Normal" defines beauty as external. Sure people say it's what's on the inside that makes you beautiful but really, our culture highly values visual beauty. This leads to a very narrow and myopic definition of beauty, which can be harmful not only to us, but to our kids. It's our job to define beauty for our kid—both the internal and external aspects.

I (Jenny) recognized the need to broaden my definition one-day, not too long after Luci's 4th birthday. We were standing in the bathroom (most of my major conversations happen in the bathroom for some reason) and Luci asked if she could curl her hair so she'd look beautiful for Daddy. While it was cute, it was also shockingly sad for me. I realized we'd only defined beauty for her, as outward appearance. Sure, we say things like you're beautiful on the inside and out, but when it came down to getting an emotional reaction from me or her Daddy, we'd been giving her big ones for curled hair and twirly dresses.

I vowed that day I would begin calling out beautiful inward characteristics as much as I do visual attributes. When Luci is kind to her brother, I tell her she is beautiful. When Luci is friendly to a new kid at the park, I tell her that loving and welcoming words are beautiful. I want her to believe, and know, that beauty is both character and outward appearance. I don't want to downplay her love of beautiful things like dresses and jewelry, those things are beautiful and so is the body she's been given. Along with that, I want to give her a more holistic definition that includes a multi-faceted description.

It's a privilege to be the main influencers in how our kids see their beauty. If we start at an early age, our kids will believe what we tell them for the rest of their lives. We can make a difference!

Michelle Smith, mom of 3 kids ages 13-19 told us her mom excelled in teaching what true beauty was about. She told us her mom literally would speak truth about beauty over her. Starting at an early age her mom would make statements like,

> *"You have beautiful lips. She would walk past me and pop my booty and say, 'You are so solid. I LOVE it.' To this day my lips and butt are my two favorite things. Solid would be perceived as a bad word I think today. It's so good though because I am thick. I do have a big butt. I am short and curvy and always have been. Always will be—even 30 pounds up or down. My butt and lips are still my favorite features."*

These statements began shaping Michelle's beliefs about her body from an early age. When she hit 7 and began to look at her body she believed it was beautiful because her mom *"Didn't tell me I was beautiful as much as she made me feel it."*

3. Thoughtful Responses to Awkward Observations

It was Spring and I (Sarah) stood in the fitting room trying on swimsuits. Being in the throes of this book and thinking a lot about what I'm communicating, I felt kinda scared! The fitting room can be a discouraging place and I didn't want to communicate a damaging message to my kids who were with me. I said to our kids (3 and 6 at the time), *"I'm going to try on 2 swimsuits and I want you to tell me which is your favorite."*

I tried on the first one. As I looked at it, I noticed that it was gapping in the front and showing that I have no chest at all, it was bunchy and the cut of the suit wasn't very flattering to my butt or thighs. I kept these observations to myself and had a total poker face the entire time (kids read facial expressions!) Jackson crinkled his nose and said, *"No. I don't like that suit. I don't like the color and it doesn't look very comfortable."*
Right on, son. Right on.

I tried on the second one. I liked this suit. It had enough padding that it looked like I had some boobs without going overboard. There was ruching in the front, which is forgiving around the midsection and the cut was fine for my butt and thighs. Jackson chimed in, *"Mom, I like this one!"* I asked him why he liked it and he said, *"I like how bunchy it is and it feels really soft so it must be comfortable, right, Mom?"*

My mind was swirling a thousand thoughts a second about what to say, how to stay neutral and non-condemning, but also honest about how I felt about my body in this swimsuit. *"Bud, you're right, it's super soft, and the best part is that I feel super comfortable in it. When I'm running around the pool making sure you and Em are safe and swimming with you, I think this suit will do a great job. I think the details on the suit are pretty, don't you?"*

I chose to focus on the attributes of the suit instead of the deficiencies of my body.

Leslie Sim, a clinical psychologist and director of Mayo Clinic's eating disorders program said in an interview, *"Moms are probably the most important influence on a daughter's body image. Even if a mom says to the daughter, 'You look so beautiful, but I'm so fat,' it can be detrimental."* [xxii]

And yet, there are countless moments in mothering where we're put in awkward situations that we're unprepared for.

I (Jenny) was in the shower with Luci one day when I noticed her looking at my belly button and then looking back at hers. She was clearly noticing a difference. I got mine pierced in college and took it out with pregnancy. My belly button now looks like a one-eyed, sad cyclops. In that moment I had no idea what to do. I didn't have to say anything, she hadn't asked a question or verbalized her observation, but I felt this tension of wanting to say something. Instead I just rinsed my hair out.

Since then, I had an interesting conversation with Jennifer, a mom of 3 boys, about sex and body image. She told me she uses the opening, *"Have you noticed,"* to set up a conversation about body changes and the differences between men and women.

Looking back in that shower scenario, it would've been a great opportunity for me to say, *"Have you noticed that my belly button looks different than yours?"* I don't want to hide my body from my kids. I want to embrace all the changes and treat them as natural. I also don't want to lie to my kids and say I feel beautiful and awesome about myself, if it isn't the case. So this question *"Have you noticed…"* gives us a way to talk about these things in a neutral way. This question acknowledges that there is a difference and makes it okay to have a conversation about it.

When our kids ask us a question, or make a statement about our bodies, it's okay to pause and not answer or respond immediately. It's even okay to say, *"I don't know, I'll have to think about that."* When we pause, we're able to assess what we'd like to intentionally communicate to our kids in that moment. A conversation where this happens might look like:

Awesomely Observant Kid: *"Mom, you've got a lot of wrinkles on your belly."*

You: *"Good observation. I do have a lot of wrinkles on my belly."*

DONE. Unless they go further.

Curious Kid: *"Mom, why do you have wrinkles on your belly?"*
You: *"I got them while you were growing in my belly."*

DONE. Unless **you** wanna go further.

Awesome You: *"These wrinkles remind me of how much I love you and how big a gift you are to me."*

You weren't dishonest. You may hate those wrinkles. You may wear tight clothes just to suck those wrinkles in and hide them. Or wear loose clothes to hide them. Either way, you love your kids and those wrinkles remind you of your greatest gifts.

4. Set the Emotional Tone

I (Jenny) recently experienced the heartache of a miscarriage. During the few days when it was happening, I sat in bed heavy with overwhelming emotions. I shared with the kids that I was sad and interestingly, I noticed everything I emoted ended up being absorbed and reflected back by the kids. Luci became unloving and harsh. Levi became whiney and forlorn. In their own ways, they were picking up what I was laying down. Sadness. Confusion. Pain. In those moments without even realizing it, we were teaching them how to handle difficult emotions.

David Code, child-development researcher and author of *Kids Pick up on Everything: How Parental Stress Is Toxic To Kids*, believes our levels of stress, in any given area of life, can alter our kids' development. He's been featured in big time stuff like *The New York Times*, *Forbes*, and *The Wall Street Journal*. He looks at neuroscience and kids from more than 20 countries to claim some pretty startling stuff.

Code found a link between a parent's stress level and their kid's cognitive, social, and emotional development. Kids who grew up in high-stress environments, no matter how loving and positive the parents were, seemed to show delayed or unhealthy development patterns. Code was fascinated to watch children of high powered and successful CEOs struggle with ADHD or getting into college. A loving parent who tells their kid they're awesome and made perfectly, aren't the determining factor in how their kids develop. It has more to do with the peace within the home. Not fake peace. Not *"Let's all put on a happy face even though we're going through a terrible time"* peace. Real peace that genuinely feels the good and the bad and helps our kids learn how to lean in to these feelings and process them in a healthy and beneficial way. How we choose to engage in our emotions sets the tone for how our kids will handle their feelings.

As moms we struggle with our fears because many of us were never taught how to process difficult experiences. The whole idea of facing our negative emotions sounded crazy back in Chapter 5 because the schemas we developed to handle them are non-existent. It's much easier to create effective emotional folders at a young age than to struggle through creating them as adults.

We Fail...A Lot

For every victory we celebrate in getting it right with our kids, there are 10 failures where we didn't get it right. It's tough work and it's worthy work. Failure means we've taken a risk and attempted something, which in our opinion, is actually a victory. The more we try the better chance we have of getting it right. My (Jenny's) dad used to say this really cheesy thing to me when I played basketball in high school. I actually think Wayne Gretzky the hockey player said it first but don't tell my dad. He used to say, "*Jenny, you miss 100% of the shots you don't take.*"

So true, Dad (and Wayne). Not trying is failure. Trying with the chance to do it better the next time is victory.

Look, we all screw up, and you're probably thinking of some stupid stuff you've said to your kids. What we all really need is a fist bump and a "*get back in the game.*" The worst thing we could do is to sit on the parenting sidelines; our kids need us in the game. If you're reading this book, you obviously want to learn, to gain insight and wisdom in how to do this, and that, friends, is success.

Recap

- ✓ Being a parent is ridiculous sometimes—our kids think we have nipples the size of Texas—they notice everything. Every. Single. Thing.
- ✓ Our job of *leading* our kids is not so ridiculous. It is critical.
- ✓ Speaking truth over our kids will help them with their own body image and will impact future generations. No pressure.
- ✓ Since kids learn most powerfully through their surroundings, we need to tune in to what messages we are sending them (verbal and non).

✓ We covered 4 ways to help our kids create positive body image:
   1. Celebrate a growth mindset.
   2. Redefine beauty.
   3. Give thoughtful responses to awkward observations.
   4. Set the emotional tone.

✓ Tools for talking to our kids about our bodies (or theirs):

   → "Have you noticed?"
   → "I don't know, I'll have to think about that…"
   → Stay neutral, stick to the facts, and muster the best poker face possible.
   → "Your compassion, generosity, kind words, (insert noun) is so beautiful."

Action Steps
Journal or Discuss

Before we can help lead our kids we have to lead ourselves. Like the challenge from our last chapter, this has an interactive component that starts with our personal journey and then invites our kids into it.

✹ To start, spend some time answering the following questions on your own.

Beautiful looks like:
Beautiful feels like:
Beautiful thinks like:

- Now think about your kids, how have you heard them define beauty?

- How would you like to hear your kids define beauty?

- What are some things you'd like to start doing to help your kids find contentment with their own bodies?

- What are some things you'd like to stop doing in your beauty conversations with your kids?

Next, remember how we scheduled intentional time with our partners? Let's do the same thing with our kids. Schedule one-on-one time with each of your kids. Write it in the calendar and make it a priority. During this time have fun *and* find a way to ask the following questions:

→ What does beautiful look like?
→ What does it feel like?
→ How does someone who is beautiful think?
→ Do you feel beautiful?
→ Do you think Mommy feels beautiful? Why or why not?
→ Who is the most beautiful person you know and why?

No matter what their answers are this conversation gives you 2 things. First, it gives you a baseline for where to start in leading your kids towards contentment. Second, it gives you an open door to have future conversations. Don't feel like you have to correct their answers or teach them everything they need to know about contentment in this one conversation. If we listen and love well in this initial talk, a door of tremendous influence will be opened to us in our relationship with our kids. Patience is our friend and allows us to be influencers in our kid's lives—and what a beautiful and great honor it is.

So schedule it. Go get some good grub. And have some great conversations with your kids. Boy, we'd love to hear the goodness that'll come.

8

Who's In Your Bunker?

The friend who can be silent with us in a moment of despair or confusion, who can stay with us in an hour of grief and bereavement, who can tolerate not knowing, not curing, not healing, and face with us the reality of our powerlessness, that is a friend who cares.

HENRI J.M. NOUWEN

How ya doing, friend? We packed a lot into the last chapter. Hope your head isn't exploding. (Truth be told, every time we edited chapters 6 and 7 we had to take a nap.)

So far in this book, we've identified what deceives, distracts, and disconnects us, we've looked at our inner journey, and we've laughed and cried our way through our bodily changes. We've also kicked fear in the teeth and reconnected with our partners while also journeying through the overwhelming world of parenting kids who'll grow up to define beauty a little different than we did. Dang, ladies. We've done a lot.

But we're not done yet. There's one more relational dynamic we've gotta discuss. We all have friends who either energize us or suck the life out of us. You have those friends. We have those friends and we all know it. Let's get honest and see how they can influence our lives.

The Jewish King Solomon was known by the nation of Israel to have the gift of wisdom. Many of his writings are included in the Christian Bible, including this one, *"He who walks with wise men will be wise, but the companion of fools will suffer harm."*[xxiii]

So how do we walk with wise friends and avoid the fools?

First, we need to identify the ways in which friendships can negatively impact us.

Our community—or the people our lives intersect with on a regular basis—can hold us back in two major ways:

1. By pulling us into groupthink.
2. By creating false intimacy.

Let's dig deeper into these 2 pitfalls and uncover some tools we can use to identify crappy friends.

Groupthink

How many of us have heard and probably used the old adage, "*If Susie jumped off a bridge, would you?*" while growing up. Yeah. We did. Peer pressure was a legit thing when we were kids (and is even crazier today.) And it didn't stop when we became parents; it just began to look a little differently.

A majority of women from our survey talked about the external pressures they feel from their peers. We've also personally experienced it in our lives and we bet you have too.

Amy, mom of 2, said about her post-baby body, "*I felt terrible, like why can't I be one of those women that just have the baby and be [sic] normal again.*"

We'd like to meet "those" women who just had the baby and are "normal" again. It's a damn lie. A damn tragedy and a damn shame that anyone believes there are women who aren't changed after baby. But we fall for it hook, line, and sinker. We believe that lie, because somewhere in our battle, we've let someone into our bunker who claims they've had the baby and are "normal" again. (End rant)

As moms we're not facing the nanny-nanny-boo-boo childhood taunting peer pressure to look a certain way. We're facing a *"subtle"* cultural influence from our peer group and it has a sophisticated name; it's called groupthink.

In 1972, psychologist Irving Janis coined the term "groupthink." [xxiv] Essentially what he said was when we're part of a group, we run the risk of not thinking or choosing for ourselves, rather we make decisions based on what the group thinks or feels, even if we disagree with these choices.

Earlier in the book, we looked at our culture and how the media and social media communicate certain messages. When we slow down and pay attention, we can easily see how they're some of the most powerful originators of groupthink. However, they're not as powerful as the people our lives connect with on a daily basis. Look at how you dress, where you eat, where you live, and the hobbies you have. Most likely the group you choose to spend the most time with influences those. The more time you spend, the more you begin to look like the people you surround yourself with. If we're not slowing down to examine the messages and compare them to our own values, beliefs, and convictions, we subtly begin to shift from independent thinker to group thinker.

What this means for us moms, is that hanging out with friends who are consistently unhappy with their bodies, negatively talk about it, or have an unhealthy fixation with their bodies can lead us to becoming the same way. It doesn't necessarily lead us to thinking the same way but we end up making decisions and taking action on things we don't really believe in.

Conversely, groupthink can also be amazingly encouraging and powerful. When we choose to surround ourselves with other women who choose joy and embrace positivity, we too begin to shift that direction and make those same choices for our own lives. We all have limited time resources and investing in these types of positive thinking relationships can help us grow.

False Intimacy

Every so often I (Jenny) do a social media purge. It's mostly driven by annoyance at someone I've never met friend requesting me. Then I get all irritated and decide to unfollow or unfriend anyone I don't have conversations with on a regular basis. But I still have a lot of "friends." Only they're not really friends, they're people it *feels* like I know, when in reality, I don't know them any better than I know how to speak Flemish. What I do have with them is this thing called false intimacy.

In addition to groupthink, community also poses another danger to our freedom in luring us into false intimacy. If intimacy is being known, with all our faults and talents, then false intimacy is the *appearance or false belief* of being fully known. And like we said in Chapter 6, true intimacy can only be created with vulnerability and consistent connection.

In Michael Ignatieff's, *The Need of Strangers*, Ignatieff looks at the cultural climate that has led to a disconnect among people. In his book he says, *"We think of belonging as permanence, yet all our homes are transient. Who still lives in the house of their childhood? Who still lives in the neighborhood [sic] where they grew up? Our belonging is no longer to something fixed, known, and familiar; but to an electric and heartless creature eternally in motion."*

Ignatieff is saying our culture doesn't lend itself to deep relational connections, rather it demands our constant movement and disconnection. Our ability to connect instantly to a mass of people often times lures us into a false sense of being known and cared for.

When I (Jenny) struggled through my miscarriage, very few of my 900-something Facebook friends showed up or even knew about it. Or when three of us had the flu over Christmas, none of my Instagram friends showed up with soup and a movie. Think back to your last tough life moment. How many of your Twitter followers showed up to eat ice cream with you? Social connection isn't the same thing as being cared for and fully known.

We believe personal growth happens most powerfully in the context of authentic relationships. This change can happen in isolation, but we believe it's extremely hard and happens rarely.

Carlin Flora, author of *Friendfluence*, says this about the effect of friendships[xxv]:

> *"It's true that just being with a friend lowers our blood pressure. Other health effects of solid friendships are among the most surprising; friends can help us break bad habits or lose weight, simply because we are so driven to adapt the values and behaviors of those in our social group. Laughing with friends can increase physical pain thresholds by about ten percent. Friends enhance your intelligence (since you're comfortable with them you're more likely to freely share insights until something brilliant surfaces) and they can even save your wits. Elderly people with active social lives are much less likely to experience cognitive decline and dementia than those without."*

We need deep friendships or we'll get dumb and die. Okay, maybe not quite that extreme, but we need friends in order to thrive. Our cultural norm leads us to believe we're deeply connecting when in reality we're not. It's become commonplace to communicate through shortened mediums rather connect in face-to-face relationships. This leaves us with relationships that "feel" real since the frequency of posting and interacting increases, but in actuality we're not availing ourselves to being fully known. **Social media interaction isn't a substitute for authentic friendships.**

In the communication theory realm, there are two words theorists often use to describe relationships, depth and breadth. (It's actually called the Theory of Social Penetration…hehehehehehe.) Depth is how vulnerable

(honest and deep) those relationships go and breadth is
how broad they are.

I (Jenny) have a set of running friends. When I have a
question about running, shoes, sports bras, or peeing in
my pants when I run, I ask my running friends. When we
run, we often talk about upcoming races, the newest
article we've read on calories, and what pace we'd like to
run next year. They're very narrow and surface
conversations. The depth is shallow and the breadth is
narrow because we typically only talk about one subject:
running.

However, I do have some running friends who I feel
comfortable talking about broader topics with and can
discuss them more deeply. With a few of my friends, our
running chats sometimes include how our marriages are
doing, what we're struggling with, and might even
include crying on a log in the woods. The breadth of that
relationship is wide because we talk all areas of life and
the depth is deep because we're being emotionally
vulnerable with one another. I experience deep healing
and growth in the midst of those conversations. These
are my people. We can run together, cry together, laugh
together, challenge each other, and speak truth to each
other when we need to hear it. I can talk to them about
anything and everything, deep and wide. And when I
need a kick in the pants, they willingly give it. I
experience growth in my life because of these friends.

Variety is awesome and having lots of different types of
relationships is sweet, not all of our friends need to be

BFFs. Let's just make sure we do invest in a few relationships that are deep and meaningful. This balance will bring us more enjoyment and fulfillment in life.

Who's In Your Space?

As we seek to walk with wise friends and avoid the fools, a tool we can leverage is looking at our relationships through the lens of space. Joseph Meyer, in his book *Search to Belong,* claims we create belonging in 4 main spaces, and believes it is important to experience relationship and true connection in each of them. This relational framework offers us a tool to bring balance into our lives. If we miss a space, Meyer says we'll struggle with our sense of overall belonging. Let's take a look at each of these areas.

Public Space

I (Jenny) graduated from the University of Kentucky. No matter where we are, if I see a person wearing UK gear, I know I can connect because we belong to the same social space. We don't self-disclose a lot of information to each other and will most likely talk about this year's recruiting class and last year's performance. It's pretty shallow and surface, but we belong to the same public space and that offers us a quick connection.

JENNY BAKER & SARAH BLIGHT

Social Space

This space is full of relationships where we give
snapshots of our lives while also guarding our image.
Most often this space might hold our relationship with
our neighbors or our hairstylist. These are also the
relationships we're testing out to see if we want to
connect more deeply. The moms groups we go to or the
volunteer groups we're a part of might fit into this
category. This space becomes kinda like a "testing"
period.

Personal Space

If someone passes the social space test, we might move
into the personal space. This is where our self-disclosure
becomes deeper and broader. Our relationships in this
space usually are stable and deep enough that even if we
haven't spoken to this friend in a period of time, reconnecting is easy and comfortable. With these friends
we share most of our lives but not so much it makes the
other person uncomfortable.

Intimate Space

Finally, there's our intimate space. This space involves
our relationship with people like our spouse, best friend,
mom, or sister. These relationships are completely open
and without constraint. These people know our strengths
and weaknesses, and love us and value us fully. We've
often given these people freedom to expose areas of
unhealthy (emotional, physical, mental) behaviors in our
lives and trust them enough to be fully honest. Here is
where the love is real and it's unconditional. It's no

surprise that it's in this intimate space where most of our life transformation happens in a powerful way. When we're in a place of total openness, trust, and honesty, our ability to wrestle through the negative in our lives and move to a place of healing and growth becomes most effective. We *need* these relationships to help us move closer towards contentment with our bodies.

Most often our public and social space relationships don't require much effort, while our personal and imitate relationships do, which is why we typically have a lot more "acquaintances" than deep friendships. Yet it's in these personal and intimate spaces where we move towards health, balance, and personal growth. Even if the vulnerability seems risky and unsafe, or the time commitment seems too high, we believe these relationships are critical to experiencing a positive journey.

Boundaries

"Personally, I'm sure you're a delightful person. But unless I know you, DO NOT ring my doorbell or knock.
I already know who I'm voting for.
Seriously, leave us alone."

(Handmade sign on Jenny's front door after bringing Luci home from the hospital.)

I (Jenny) remember the moment we brought her home. I didn't anticipate the entire neighborhood walking down the street to meet our newest member. I didn't anticipate the neighbor kids—with all their germs and runny noses— to want a peek at the new babe. If only I'd anticipated a little more I wouldn't have lost my shit that February afternoon.

I was feeling BIG feelings and then all these people descended on my house like seagulls to bread crumbs and I freaked out. In a short and tense tone I told everyone the baby was sleeping and we needed space and they needed to come back later. I knew when everyone got quiet I'd probably gone a little far. Problem was I didn't care. I just needed space.

The only way I knew how to communicate this was by posting a sign on my front door for all curious visitors to see. Did I go too far? Perhaps. Did I care? Nope. I needed some helpful boundaries.

Dr. Henry Cloud and Dr. John Townsend have written more books on the topic of boundaries than any other authors on the subject. These guys define a boundary as, *"A boundary is a personal property line that marks those things for which we are responsible. In other words, boundaries define who we are and who we are not."*[xxvi]

We just talked about groupthink and false intimacy and now it's time for us to talk about how to manage these relationships. We can't cut everyone that doesn't make us feel super duper positive about ourselves out of our lives. What we *can* do is learn how to manage them.

I (Sarah) grew up in a home with a parent who had debilitating, chronic depression. As a 9, 10, 11-year-old, I would often find myself in the role of "parent" to that parent. I would worry, pray, comfort, console, and try to bear the burden of that depression. It wasn't until many, many years later that I realized the impact that had on me as a child—I could probably write an entire book on that alone. Suffice it to say, there was no boundary present between us. The result was that I took ownership of many things that I had no business owning. I was a child doing an adult's work and eventually it broke me. As a result, I developed the habit of taking responsibility for many things that were not mine and feeling a ton of guilt in the process. The upside though is that later in life this ultimately led me to figuring out how important, healthy, and comforting boundaries are in relationships, and to experience freedom and joy within them. Boundaries are freeing because they remove the grey areas and allow for open and authentic relationships.

My (Jenny's) dad tells a story of a man who owed his partner a lot of money. One night he was up pacing in his bedroom when his wife asked what was wrong. He confessed he owed his partner the money and didn't know how he would pay. His wife quickly picked up the phone, called his partner, told him they didn't have the money, and hung up. She then looked at her husband and said, *"Now it's Randy's problem, come back to bed."*

Another one of my dad's classics is telling me everyone has a monkey on their back and they're always trying to give it to someone else. He then admonishes me by telling me not to let others put their monkey on my back.

Get the picture?

Unless we think it, feel it, and own it for ourselves, **we aren't responsible for another's opinion of our lives**. Our weight, our appearance, our clothes, our body is no one else's business.

Can you tell this fires us up?

Deep breath. And now we transition…

Author Mark Manson says this about boundaries:

> "*Setting strong personal boundaries are not a cure-all for your relationship woes (or your lost keys). In fact, they're more of a side effect of having a healthy self-esteem and a general low level of neediness with people around you. Boundaries work both ways: they create emotional health and are created by people with emotional health. They are something you can start working on today with the people close to you and you'll begin to notice a difference in your self-esteem, confidence, emotional stability, and so on.*" [xxvii]

Boundaries help us own our feelings and not take on the messages and beliefs of others (like friends, family, acquaintances, pesky media, retailers, and others who communicate their personal agenda.)

Boundaries are a great idea in any and all relationships, not just the ones that are potentially unhelpful. But for the purposes of our book, we'll focus on setting boundaries in a relationship that might be leading us towards discontentment with our post-baby bodies.

Let's check out three ways we can implement boundaries:
1. Our words
2. Our time
3. Our disclosure level.

Our Words

Boundaries are the product of courage and confidence. When we're certain about our worth and value, we're able to embrace who we are and reject what pushes us into being someone we aren't. Words are tremendously helpful in establishing boundaries and yet require a tremendous amount of gumption.

Verbally disagreeing with a statement someone has made is never comfortable or easy. It takes a significant amount of energy and grace to stand on an opposing side. Basically it's the polar opposite of groupthink. And yet, it's the start of seeing ourselves as strong and independent women.

I (Jenny) found myself in a women's group one fall, listening to a sex therapist talk about having a healthy sex life. There were several comments made about the importance of the visual aspect and the need to make sure we were wearing sexy clothes for our partners. I found my mind drifting to a place of anger and inadequacy again, thinking back to the last time I could remember busting out my sexy nighties. And then I stopped. I didn't really believe and agree with what this

woman was saying and I began to dissect what I was
hearing:

- I didn't agree that all women and all men are
  visual, and that sexy lingerie was the key to a
  healthy sex life.

- I didn't believe I should feel ashamed if I
  preferred having the room pitch black and not
  putting clothes on, since they'd be coming off
  anyway.

- I didn't believe that because I hated how my old
  lingerie fit and therefore didn't wear it, that my
  sex life was doomed. I mean, I still wear my
  nursing tank tops to bed and I haven't nursed a
  kid in years!

- And I didn't believe anyone should prescribe
  what healthy sex looked like for me.

That's a lot of disbeliefs.

As I realized what message was trying to jump all up in
my mind, I found myself sitting taller in my chair. My
heart rate picked up, I leaned forward in my chair, and
my face started to get hot. I was getting angry! So I took
a deep breath and jumped in with a statement of
freedom mainly for me, but also in hopes of rescuing
other women. *"I think I see things a little differently,"* I said.
"I'm not sure I agree with the statement that to have a healthy sex

life I need to be wearing sexy lingerie." I continued on, "*There are other factors that seem to be more of a priority for me.*"

The room was quiet for a moment, and then the floodgates opened and several other women jumped in with similar comments.

It wasn't that I disagreed and needed to be right or be heard, it was that what was being shared was being presented as fact, for everyone. There may be moments as you've read this book or even now, where we mention something that you're not sure you agree with…which is **great** because the purpose of this book is to create a space for each of us to evaluate what we're thinking and feeling and come to our own conclusions. We also have the opportunity to become conscious consumers. As we gain knowledge and experience from this book and our life, let's think about what it is we're consuming from ALL influencing factors and feel the freedom and confidence to speak up when we disagree. Words can be powerful when used with courage and gentleness.

Our Time

Time is our most valuable commodity and something we'll never get back once we give it. This means investing it wisely is important. When we spend time with a person or group it can be helpful to evaluate how we're feeling. A few questions to ask ourselves are:
-Am I feeling positive?
-Do I feel the freedom to disagree with those thoughts?
-Can I fully express myself in this situation?

If we find ourselves in a relationship that leaves us feeling uncared for, not heard, not peaceful, and downright anxious, it's time to limit our exposure to that person or group.

Our Disclosure Level

The last boundary we find helpful is the boundary of disclosure or how deeply we share ourselves with others. Our culture, especially social media, demands a level of self-exposure. Opening up our lives to the public is the price we pay to stay connected, and it can come with a big penalty if not thoughtfully managed. It's important to recognize every group and every person doesn't need to know everything about us.

My (Jenny's) parents used to paraphrase a Bible quote that says something like, *"Don't share your pearls with pigs."* It sounds ridiculous but holds deep truth for me. Pearls are valuable. They're precious and beautiful, and clearly pigs wouldn't understand their value. Dad would tell me there are things that are valuable and beautiful to me, like my busted blood vessels on my face I got from pushing so hard with my first baby, or the birth stories of both my kids, and there are certain people who won't understand their value and worth.

If I share those priceless treasures with the wrong people, I'll most likely leave feeling hurt and as if my beautiful "pearls" have been trampled on. There are things I don't want the world to know and things the world doesn't need to know. We don't have to be open books for everyone.

Conversely, there are people to share my "pearls" with. There's a level of authenticity that comes with time and trust. This vulnerability is good and necessary for deep friendships to happen. When someone actively wants to invest in our lives and we feel loved and cared for by them, deep self-disclosure is life giving and this boundary becomes unnecessary.

FYI

One word of caution—especially to those of you who are new to this whole idea of boundaries—remember that you are setting boundaries for yourself so that you know what is yours to take ownership of and what's not. This will upset people, especially the master manipulators and energy takers. While you were once a person they could control or be careless with their words around, as you take that power back and give them back their damn monkey, you force them to start taking ownership of what's theirs; and they won't be happy about it. So just anticipate that creating boundaries in your relationships will most likely end some of them. To which we say "buh-bye." Because the freedom we experience is well worth the pain of losing master manipulators and energy takers.

Phew.

What a chapter. We're pretty passionate about healthy relationships that encourage and inspire us. Hopefully you have some of these in your life. If you don't, fear not, if you look for them you'll find them. It may take some time but there are amazing people in the world who want to be in your life and will most definitely want you in theirs.

And because they'll want you in their life, we're required to look at our own selves and answer the question, am I that kind of friend to others? Being a giver and not just a taker lends itself to fulfilling relationships that become an extension of our contentment. Get a few good ones and man, you'll feel like you can conquer the world.

Recap

- ✓ Who we hang out with matters. Walk with the wise, avoid the fools.
- ✓ Two ways friendships can negatively impact us are groupthink and false intimacy.
- ✓ It's important to have relationships that are both deep and wide.
- ✓ The four spaces: public, social, personal, and intimate help us balance our relationships.

✓ Pursuing and protecting relationships that lead us
where we want to go requires us to establish
healthy boundaries.
✓ We can establish boundaries through our words,
our time, and how much we share with our
friends.
✓ We will tick people off when we start using
boundaries.

Action Steps
Journal or Discuss

✂ Think back on the four areas of space: public,
private, social, and intimate. Using those four
categories, list the people who most frequently share
your life space.

Public:

Private:

Social:

Intimate:

⌘ Now, thinking through each of those relationships, answer the following questions:

→ After spending time with them, am I feeling positive?
→ Do they share their opinions with me?
→ Do I feel respected if I disagree with them?
→ If I don't agree with them, do I feel valued for what I do believe?
→ Does this relationship get me closer or further away from experiencing contentment in my life?
→ What kind of friend am I? (Would I wanna be my own friend?)

⌘ Based on your answers, who would you like to:

→ Start spending more time with?
→ Stop spending time with?
→ Continue spending time with?

9

Competitors or Teammates?

Friendship…is born at the moment when one man says to another
"What! You too? I thought that no one but myself…"

C.S. LEWIS – *The Four Loves*

Franklin and I (Jenny) have had the privilege of traveling and helping others cross-culturally. We've invested our time and skills towards building into places like Haiti, Peru, and Africa. I very vividly remember a trip we took to Namibia, Africa. We traveled to several remote villages to offer medical care to those who didn't have easy access. The first day as we began seeing people, it got really confusing, really quickly. Kids were running around everywhere and the minute a baby or toddler would start crying, a woman would pick her up, pop out her boob and begin to nurse her. My western culture way of thinking, told me that was the child's mom….and boy,

171

was I wrong. When one of the women came to the intake table nursing a babe, I told her I thought her baby was beautiful. She (and all the other women around her) promptly began to laugh at me. Turns out the baby belonged to her friend, whose boob was already taken by another kid. She, along with the entire community, co-mothered. Every child belonged to every parent. Discipline, comfort, feeding, and love were shared. It was teamwork at it's finest.

In our Western culture, bustin' out a boob and feeding any hungry, cranky baby within arm's reach would create quite a stir. But man, what a beautiful illustration of women.

We're resilient, capable, beautiful, protective, nurturing, and we are so strong. We are women!!!

However, like we've worked hard at doing this entire journey, if we want personal growth, we have to look at reality. And this one is a bitch. *Cinderella, Snow White, Little Mermaid,* and so many other movies tell our culture this ugly tale: women opposing women.

If we get real we can all say we've...

Compared
Judged
Hurt
Rejected or
Resented...other women.

Author Susan Shapiro Barash agrees.[xxviii]

> *"We need to finally admit there's a problem. To finally say, 'hello, can everyone admit that whether it's your friend telling you she's engaged or pregnant or her kid got into Harvard or whatever she tells you that seems so incredibly close to a goal of yours that you haven't achieved, to stop secretly seething."*

Our quiet discord comes from an unmet need deep inside our hearts. We see other women we think have something we want but don't have, and it creates an inner turmoil that we're ill equipped to navigate. Like fear and the other emotions we've written about, these feelings of jealousy and inadequacy compel us towards action that, most of the time, is destructive.

Author Victoria Fedden genuinely writes about her struggle with this opposition[xxix].

> *"Pretty soon, I didn't even recognize myself. Women I'd once loved to spend time with, I now hated. It was almost like I enjoyed hating them, like being mean to them leveled the field. Being nasty didn't make me feel better, and when my anger finally boiled over and I publicly lashed out at a friend for leaving her daughter for yet another whirlwind, adult vacation, she told me off for being judgmental and unfriended me permanently."*

We'd say a majority of us could relate to those feelings.

Yet oddly, not too long ago, we depended on each other for our very survival and lived in extremely close proximity. Women worked together, gathering and preparing food, and taking care of all the details of daily life. They shared knowledge and support during childbirth and had no choice but to be in constant contact for the mere fact that it meant survival (and in some cultures, it's still this way).

Presently, in our first-world culture, we don't seem to need each other. All we really need is electricity, the Internet, and a couple of machines and we're all set to rule our roost.

Not only is it possible to be a solo mom, we'd even say in our first-world society, "normal" pushes us to see each other as competitors rather than teammates.

If we can get out of our personal realities and congregate for a sec, we would quickly realize we all really do want the same things. Really. At the core of who we are as moms we all agree we want health, safety and freedom. We want equality. We desire opportunities. We yearn to feel strong, capable and confident about our lives and we hope for the same for our kids. Yet, we have very different beliefs, convictions, approaches, and values which lead us there (or don't) and somehow, as women, we have come to be threatened by these different approaches. Why? Why do we care so much what choices others make? Does it impact us in some way? Does it make our job harder as women in some way? What gives?

With a little teamwork we can raise the water level under everyone's boat rather than leave each other stranded on the shore of jealousy and isolation. Let's talk a bit about what this solidarity requires.

Take A Risk

December of 2014 found Jenny and I together at a local Cincinnati park, desperately trying to play our kids to an early bedtime. Our paths had crossed sporadically over the past several years as we both had kids, raised kids, and managed to be working moms living in 2 different states. Our work was different and yet common. We both helped people personally grow through different seasons of life and enjoyed seeing others experience personal triumph. Despite having both experienced a small level of our own personal achievements in book writing, public leadership, and keeping our kids alive, we found ourselves talking in the park, about an area of our lives we both kept hidden, our body after babies.

Jenny suggested my next book be about this topic and I quickly laughed, hiding the fear that violently arose in my heart. She shared her struggle and journey with her post-body, one I never imagined she had. As our play date in the park came to an end, the seed had been planted and sat germinating over the winter, until that fear and the idea became overwhelmingly compelling.

My fear came from believing I was alone in this fight, from believing I was the only one who peed in her pants when she sneezed and felt insecure about her body. And yet, the more I sat in those feelings, the more I realized I wanted this to stop for all women; the more I wanted us to believe a different story. And so, I reached out to Jenny and we decided this book had to be written...together.

Oh ladies, you should've been in the initial conversations around how this book would look, talk about different approaches. From the initial conversations, it made more sense for us to each write our own book. Instead, we took the risk and forged on together, until we had our first chapter deadline.

When the time came for us to read each other's drafts, we both tried to figure out how to kindly tell the other that we'd never read their version of the book in a million years. Jenny hated my light-hearted, funny, lack of research perspective and I glazed over reading Jenny's statistics, studies, and punch 'em in the gut challenges.

Let's just say that writing this book together has meant arguing, disagreeing, crying, and frustration, *and* it's also given us unspeakable joy and a deep friendship that will no doubt last the rest of our lives. It's helped us to experience first-hand why doing this together is worth it.

I (Jenny) am a better woman, mom, and wife because I took a risk and choose unity rather than individualism. Over the last 2ish years, as I've spent countless hours on the phone with Sarah, I've learned so much about myself, some good and some really ugly. She's challenged my beliefs and my faith, my commitment and my follow-through. When we first started this project I took 5 days to respond to her text messages, voice messages, and emails. After a few rounds of this she got honest with me and told me how my inattention and lack of response made her frustrated and fearful this project wasn't important to me. Hearing how this made her feel made me pay more attention to how promptly I respond to everyone in my life. I think I'm a better friend because of her honest challenges.

I (Sarah) have also gained incredible insight about myself. I've learned how my strengths and weaknesses impact my writing, as well as my relationships. Jenny's a smart cookie. Her analytical, research, knowledge-loving brain really impressed me (and sometimes led to me feeling super intimidated!). But she challenged me to step up my game. By spending time with someone who is so different than I am in many ways, I have been compelled to look at things from a different perspective. It's been neat to see how a topic, issue, or personal problem can change just from looking at it from a different angle.

As you can probably tell, we dig the wisdom of King Solomon. He wrote a whole book that's full of meaningful pieces of insight and is still relevant today. He's credited as saying, *"Iron sharpens iron, as one man sharpens another.*[xxx]*"* Taking a risk and working with each other has sharpened us as a people. We'd go as far to say that coming together, finding common ground while also allowing the not-so-common ground to shape and change us, always makes us better people.

Uniting together as women to fight the lies that break us down is worth the risk and the effort. Every. Dang. Time.

Be Inspired Not Insulted

Fedden nails it when she explains *"The root cause of my envy was surprisingly simple: I needed a break. I was bored and burnt out from parenting. I'd been stuck in my house for too long with a sick kid. That's why I became enraged when I saw my friends vacationing alone."*

Hey. Remember that perspective shift thing we talked about? Yeah. It applies here too.

Our feelings of jealousy against one another come from a poverty mentality that says, *"I don't have, I'll never have, everyone else has and I should be pitied because I don't stand a chance."* A poverty mentality ends in apathy and a stalled life.

And we say, "false."

We do have. We have choices. We have a culture with abundant resources and we have hope. As moms, we often put others above ourselves and end up losing who we're created to be. Where we once were prolific writers or managers, creators or organizers, we're now pouring everything we have into supporting everyone else's dreams and talents while ours sit in the dusty attic. We tell ourselves when the kids are older we'll get them out and dust 'em off, but that doesn't always happen.

We cease to exist and fail to acknowledge our slow decay. Then one day, we see someone else living in the fullness of who they are and we feel a cringe. Honesty would tell us that cringe is sadness and a deep desire to experience the same. Yet most often, "normal" tells us why that person doesn't deserve it and the seed of discord is sown.

Instead of being personally insulted by another's success, let's use their fortune to inspire us towards our own. Allow another's personal accomplishments to motivate you towards action that results in celebrating your friend's good fortune *and* the discovery of your own! That's goodness on top of goodness and there's enough to go around.

Self, Meet Self

You're talented, capable, beautiful, strong, and have a lot to offer this world. You're not the exception. No one got left out. We're all created with unique gifts and capabilities.

The seeds of contentment and gratitude need to be planted in soil that is rich in truth in order to enjoy their abundant, live-giving fruit. Author Therese J. Borchard writes about how to do that. [xxxi]

> *"All you need to do is to be quiet for a few hours in a peaceful setting (I suggest some woods or a nearby creek if you're not afraid of ticks), and introduce yourself to yourself. "Self, meet Self. Nice to meet you, Self." Then you guys have to become friends. How? Think about all the things you like about yourself. Get out your self-esteem file and read it."*

In 2009 when I (Jenny) was struggling with my anxiety, my self-esteem file was pretty low. I felt like everything I'd stuffed in there was garbage and not even worthy of being burned. So I turned to my intimate community. Those people in my intimate space who knew me better than anyone and I asked them to fill my self-esteem folder. I asked them to write me an email telling me how they see me and what they believe my strengths to be. When I couldn't rely on my perception, I called in for reinforcements.

Either you fill up your folder with all the good that is you or you ask someone else to fill it with truth. Either way the key is to believe and feel your extreme worth and value. When you believe that, you'll stop looking at others and longing for theirs instead.

Unlock Empathy

> *"A fight is going on inside me," said an old man to his son. "It is a terrible fight between two wolves. One wolf is evil. He is anger, envy, sorrow, regret, greed, arrogance, self-pity, guilt, resentment, inferiority, lies,*

false pride, superiority, and ego. The other wolf is good. He is joy, peace, love, hope, serenity, humility, kindness, benevolence, empathy, generosity, truth, compassion, and faith. The same fight is going on inside you."

The son thought about it for a minute and then asked, "Which wolf will win?"
The old man replied simply, "The one you feed." [xxxii]

If we want to feed the wolf of unity among us women, our key is empathy. Empathy is actually a newer word, having only been coined in 1908. It's often confused with sympathy, and yet has a completely different definition.

Sympathy would be bringing a meal, watching kids, or doing laundry for a friend who's experienced a painful loss. Empathy would be sitting next to that friend and crying with them as you feel their loss. Sympathy is feeling compassion, sorrow, or pity ,while empathy is living the emotions, ideas, or opinions of the other person. Empathy requires all of us, our thoughts, our feelings, and our time, which is why it's so important in the context of friendships.

In 56 A.D., the Jewish Apostle Paul said, *"Bless your enemies; no cursing under your breath. Laugh with your happy friends when they're happy; share tears when they're down. Get along with each other; don't be stuck-up. Make friends with nobodies; don't be the great somebody. Don't hit back; discover beauty in everyone."*[xxxiii]

Even though the English word "empathy" is relatively newer to our lexicon, the concept has been around for thousands of years. And it all comes down to the fact that empathy is a choice. We choose to get down and emotionally dirty with each other and in doing so, our capacity to encourage and support others increases dramatically. When we commit to being "all in" we become an unstoppable force. Cultivating this empathy is simple but it's not easy. It requires us to do four things:

1. Stop Comparing

"Comparison is the thief of joy."-Theodore Roosevelt.

It was summer. I (Sarah) was a sophomore in college. My car had been totaled in an accident and I was carless, which was definitely a hindrance to many things in my life, the least of which was my work schedule. My parents decided to get a new car and gifted me with their minivan, AKA "The Mothership." We're talking a 5-passenger, bluish gray, Plymouth Voyager that was a stick shift!!! Yes. It was super special like that. I was thrilled. I was giddy. I finally had wheels again. This gift got me to and from work all summer and it facilitated my social life. It was fantastic.

Fall came. It was time to go back to Miami University for my junior year. To be blunt, my school had a lot of kids who didn't have to worry as much as I did about money. Many of their families were financially better off and were able to fund their college. This was way different than my money situation, which required me to work several jobs to get my degree.

As I moved into my college house, I found myself surrounded by students driving Ford Explorers (apparently, THE SUV of choice back in the late 90s) and other cars that were far nicer than The Mothership.

My joy turned to embarrassment. My giddiness turned to envy.

I was thrilled with my ride until I saw what others had. Then it wasn't sufficient. The generous gift I received had suddenly turned into a burden. I began driving all the back roads around campus because I didn't want my classmates to see me. The comparison didn't just steal my joy, it cunningly twisted the wonderful and downgraded it to second-rate.

When we compare our lives to that of others, our gifts become burdens, our overflowing cups are now half empty. We become insecure Debbie Downers who see other women as adversaries. Our empathy is blocked by apathy.

2. Stop Assuming

George Orwell, a famous British novelist, was a police officer in British Burma during the 1920s. After completing his time in Burma, he decided to return to Britain and find out what life was like for those who were not as fortunate as he was. *"I wanted to submerge myself, to get right down among the oppressed,"* he wrote. He went undercover and dressed as a vagrant and lived on the streets of East London among the homeless. He wrote all about his experiences in his book *Down and Out in Paris and London*. Orwell experienced a life-altering shift in his beliefs, his priorities, and his relationships because of his stint as a vagrant. He saw first-hand they weren't *"drunken scoundrels,"* and forged new friendships while experiencing inequality. His choice to live in the life of a person rather than make assumptions from the outside powerfully impacted his future writing and led to much success.

It's all too easy to make assumptions about people we meet and it's even easier for these assumptions to end in judgments. Empathy says, *"I'm willing to slow down, be where you are, and assign you value."* Judgment says, *"You're not valuable enough for me to spend time thinking about your opinions, feelings, or reality."*

3. Be Interested In Others' Stories

One of the actionable parts of empathy is being interested in another's life, experiences, and their current reality. This means learning how to ask questions that give you insight into who they are. In their book *Power Questions*, Andrew Sobel and Jerold Panas write:

"Good questions are often far more powerful than answers. Good questions challenge your thinking. They reframe and redefine the problem. They throw cold water on our most dearly-held assumptions, and force us out of our traditional thinking. They
184

*motivate us to learn and discover more. They remind us of what is
most important in our lives."*

Practically speaking, open-ended questions can't be
answered with a simple yes or no, rather they require
details and explanations. Asking these types of questions
gives the other person the opportunity to self-
disclose on a deeper level. As you choose to connect
with women around you, start asking meaningful open-
ended questions as a way to unlock empathy. Sometimes
it can be hard to think of questions on the spot, so we've
included 10 questions to get you started in the journal or
discuss section at the end of this chapter.

As you ask questions and enjoy learning about new and
old friends, a great follow-up in most conversations is,
"tell me more about that." Not only does it encourage the
other person to share more, it also communicates a
connectedness to and interest in their story.

4. Be Vulnerable

What is the first thing that comes to your mind when
you read the following words?

Accessible
Defenseless
Exposed
Naked

Our first response to these words as a whole is "risky!!"
They sound like a really bad therapy session. And to
some, being defenseless, accessible and exposed *while*

naked is a nightmare. (Have you ever had a naked dream where you went to school and had no clothes on? Terrifying.)

This response makes sense considering these are synonyms to the word "vulnerable." Vulnerable is risky and scary. It means being accessible. It means being exposed. It means shedding layers of self-protection and getting down to the birthday suit...butt dimples and all.

We do believe being vulnerable—as scary as it is—draws out the same beautiful vulnerability in others. With our vulnerability, we allow others to also choose empathy.

In 2013 I (Jenny) did something I never imagined I'd ever do. Ever. Not in a million years. The idea wasn't even on my radar. I shared my health journey with about 25,000 people. Men, women, teenagers, strangers, and friends all heard the ugly, but true story of how I overcame my struggle with anorexia. It was one of the scariest things I'd ever done, and yet it was something I'd been growing towards for years.

The end result was super positive and even more terrifying.

After I spoke, I invited everyone to join me in pursuing personal and spiritual health and train for Cincinnati's Flying Pig Marathon. I thought after sharing my story, maybe a few crazy people would show up to run with me, if only out of pity. Turns out I was wrong. My vulnerability ended up motivating 1,500 people to train for a race and pursue health. We had inadvertently created Cincinnati's largest running group, which started from my willingness to share my story of brokenness, weakness, and failure, and how I had overcome it.

What's your story? What failures and successes can you share to inspire others and raise the water level under their boat? Be bold and share it! You're not alone.

Everyone has a struggle, and chances are when you begin to share yours, others will follow your lead.

There is power and freedom in vulnerability because it removes the burden of perfection and replaces it with the mantle of connection.

Phew. Well, that kind of felt like a whirlwind chapter and it felt pretty uncomfortable for us. As we faced our inner demons and looked at some of the really ugly in our hearts, we realized just how blind we could be. It's a lot easier to believe we're unifiers rather than explore our negative emotions towards other mamas. But after writing this, we're agreeing to pause the next time we cringe at another teammate. Hopefully, in this pause, we'll be better equipped to explore our own complexities instead of projecting them onto another.

Unity among us ladies can be powerful. We come together as teammates rather than competitors when we commit to doing some self-awareness work and shed the "normal" of jealousy and rejection. When we plug-in to empathy we get inspired and appreciate ourselves while feeling confident enough to be vulnerable. We strip off the proud, perfect façade and we get naked, emotionally butt-naked. We show up, we open up, and we cover ourselves with the mantle of connection and offer it to others. And when we do that, we experience something so powerful. Fighting *for* each other gives us purpose and meaning that far exceeds ourselves.

Recap

✓ We struggle against opposing each other.

✓ We all basically want the same things, which puts us on the same team.

✓ We used to depend on each other for survival, but our first-world culture of convenience means we don't have to anymore. It's killing our contentment.

✓ Unlocking empathy is key to connecting with others and it means doing 4 things:
1. Stop comparing
2. Stop assuming
3. Be interested in others
4. Be vulnerable

It's pretty straightforward. It's simple but it sure ain't easy.

Action Steps
Journal or Discuss

✂ Think about a person who creates emotional tension in your life because of your differences. Evaluate the level of value you've given them.

→ How much do they mean to you?
→ Leaving presumptions aside, what do you know about this person?

✂ Choose to schedule one-on-one time with the purpose of knowing and understanding them better. Use these questions as a conversation springboard.

1. What have you learned about yourself (since becoming a mom?)
2. What's been the most helpful piece of advice anyone has given you?
3. Who has been the biggest influencer in your life?
4. What are you passionate about?
5. Have there been any big turning points for you in the last year or so?
6. How have you thrived/succeeded lately?
7. How have you failed lately?
8. Is there an achievement or contribution that you are most proud of?

9. What's been a big challenge you've faced?
10. What's your favorite book and why?

A great follow up is "*Tell me more about that…*"

- Next, spend time thinking about a mama you'd like to encourage in her journey towards contentment.

  - → How might you do that?
  - → What aspects of your journey might be helpful for her to hear?

And then be intentional and schedule consistent time with this mama. It doesn't have to be every week. It could be once a month. Whatever works with your schedule, make it happen. You'll never know what a gift your encouragement and support will mean. Having someone fight for your freedom is humbling and inspiring.

10

Embracing Change

The secret of change is to focus all your energy not on fighting the old, but on building the new.

SOCRATES

I (Jenny) was in preschool when I learned the hard and important lesson of patiently trusting a process. I remember this experience in my life because it was kinda traumatic. My class was studying butterflies and metamorphosis and each student was sent home with a butterfly larvae. It was in a tiny container and we were told to put in on our windowsill and in a few days, a butterfly would emerge. I was enthralled with the idea of being the new owner of an impending beautiful life. I imagined my butterfly's beautiful wings and felt giddy as I thought about it hatching.

Once we got home that day, I remember taking my larvae to the bathroom, quietly closing the door, and stepping up on my stool in front of the sink. I decided my almost butterfly needed a drink of water. I was convinced if it had water, it would grow faster, and faster was definitely better.

That's when I drowned my butterfly. To my 4 year-old mind, it was horribly painful. I wasn't patient and I didn't trust the process of growth. I tried to speed it up, and in my ignorance; I killed what I deeply wanted.

See? Kinda traumatic.

As we come to a close with this book, we'd be remiss if we didn't encourage and challenge you to trust **your** process. Change takes time and patience. We've thrown a lot out there; research, personal experience, and statistics. Each of these things is helpful, yet none of them will transform us unless we're willing to settle in for the long haul. Sometimes it takes years…because change isn't one big decision. Rather, it's hundreds of small decisions added up over time. One of the kindest things we can do for you, as we end this journey together, is share with you the truth about change, and that truth starts with understanding how we learn.

How We Learn

Let's put back on our research hat for a second and build on Chapter 7—remember we covered how kids develop their schemas? Right now we'd like to look at the process of learning for adults—which is really just the process of change. This can help us set our expectations for what our journey towards contentment might look like.

While the exact origin is unknown, some people credit Noel Burch[xxxiv] with breaking down learning into 4 stages. Let's check them out.

Stage 1 is unconscious incompetence.
(I don't know.)

In this phase we're not aware that we're in need of a new skill set. We're walking through life either blissfully or painfully needing to change, but not realizing change is what we need until there's a prompt that throws us into stage 2. Kinda like a toddler who isn't potty trained. They're pretty happy sitting in poop and have no idea there's something better.

Stage 2 is conscious incompetence.
(I need to know.)

This is when we first become aware of the need to learn something new. It becomes too painful to stay where we are and we realize change is inevitable, and so we commit to learning and growing. Graduation from stage 2 to 3 requires action; we can't move unless we put a plan to our intentions. If we want to quit smoking, we stop buying cigarettes or we stay away from places we're tempted to smoke. If we want to learn how to eat healthier, we read books or blogs on nutrition. The act of doing propels us into the next phase.

Stage 3 is conscious competence.
(I know but it takes work.)

The shift from stage 2 to 3 is marked with what we call "the valley." Taking the step from doing nothing to working hard, learning, and changing can be the longest and hardest step. It's marked with feelings of defeat, pain, and frustration. It's where things get hard before they get better. If you've ever kicked a harmful habit like smoking, this is the stage where you might relapse after a few good weeks and feel like a failure. This turn can feel overwhelming and is where many abandon their quest to learn and change because of how much hard work is required.

But hang in there long enough and over time—as we continue to operate in the new behavior and thought pattern—we'll get it without the effort. When we embrace and trust the process, our new way of living becomes our everyday reality. Which leads us to the last stage.

Stage 4 is unconscious competence.
(I know and don't need to think about it.)

Think of driving a car. When we were 16 we had no idea we didn't know how to drive a car. How hard could it really be? We were unconsciously incompetent; we didn't know what we didn't know. But then we signed up for driver's education class and learned the first time we attempted to parallel park, that we were complete idiots.

So we practiced. We drove with our parents and read the driver's test manual. It took a lot of conscious thinking. We'd get in the car and have to walk ourselves through all our safety checks, buckling our seatbelts, putting our hands at 10 and 2, and taking off the emergency brake. We had to think hard about being competent drivers. And somehow, with lots of practice and white-knuckle moments with our parents and other adults, we became competent drivers (well, some of us did.) Years of that have led us to getting into a car and not thinking about any of it. We've developed an unconscious competence.

Change is possible, change is a process. Knowing what to expect can help us embrace where we are and look forward to where we can be. One of the most powerful ideas we get from the stages of learning is that **change happens when we join our vision with intentional action**.

Find Your Reference Point

In 2007, I (Jenny) had an extremely powerful "focus" lesson when I met Marilyn H. Tam. Raised in Hong Kong and subject to forced child labor, Marilyn imagined something more for her life, and as a teenager, risked it all and made her way to America to pursue her dreams. Her hard work and intentional living paid off and her resume now includes positions such as CEO of Aveda, President of Reebok, and VP of Nike. I met Marilyn at a point in my young life when I was seriously confused about my career path. I didn't know what decision to make, should I take a new job I was offered that aligned with my passions, or stay in my current position that was stable and also horrifically boring? To my young adult self it was a weighty decision with life-long consequences. Fortunately, in just a short coffee chat, I found some of the most helpful and simple life advice I'd ever received.

Marilyn's response to my conundrum started with a story about sailing. She told me when a sailboat sets out, the final destination becomes the captain's reference point; the point all other decisions are driven by. As the sailboat makes forward progress, it begins a maneuver known as tacking, which to observers looks like zigzagging. It can appear to be a futile process; the sailboat makes angled turns into the wind, sometimes even moving parallel rather than forward. This positioning allows the boat to capture the wind and move it forward. At times this movement is at a fast rate, and other times it creeps along and yet, no matter the speed, the end goal is always in sight. Throughout the journey, if the captain
remains committed to the reference point and has patience, the boat gets to its destination.

According to Marilyn, my decision making process was no different. She asked what my reference point in life was. As I poured my heart and passions out to her, she looked at me and said, *"That's your reference point. When you have a decision to make, take the path that gets you closer to that destination."* She warned me to settle in for the long haul and learn to embrace hard and patient work. Her words continue to resonate with my heart and influence my decision-making.

If our reference point is contentment, then every time we have the choice between that and a different destination like discontentment, we choose to think and feel that which moves us closer to our destination. This looks like choosing to invest time in a positive friendship and saying no to time spent in a negative one, or taking a break from social media when you start to feel a tinge of inadequacy. When you make those decisions, you make a conscious move towards your vision of contentment.

Change Isn't Just An Idea

When we couple the idea of having a focused vision *with* some practical application, then change just got a lot more probable. But, if we stay only on the vision side, we're bound to get lost at sea. The captain of a boat may know where she wants to go—but without a map—she'll end up with Tom Hanks and Wilson.

The idea of being content with our post-baby bodies sounds inviting and perhaps even simple. Yet theories and ideas are only as good as they can realistically be applied in our lives. For example, we might be inspired with the idea to do weekly meal planning before we hit the grocery store. However, if we don't intentionally think and create a plan, our idea remains just that, an idea. To buy into and get excited about a vision, without being able to actually execute it, isn't inspiring; it's quite the opposite. We feel defeated, inadequate, angry, and ashamed.

I (Jenny) love to sew. My mom made my childhood clothes, and in junior high I followed in her footsteps and took sewing lessons. One afternoon after having Luci, Mom and I were looking at some pictures of me at summer camp as a kid, when I noticed the cute outfit I was wearing. Mom reminded me she had sewn it and I immediately got swept away in a tidal wave of nostalgia. It was this sentimentality that led me to ask for a sewing machine that year for Christmas. Along with my new machine, I bought several beautiful patterns and fabric to make a few cute dresses for Luci. That afternoon I tucked them away in the basement with a plan to setup a sewing table and get to work.

That was 6 years ago and I haven't touched the patterns since the day I bought them. I love the idea of sewing, but I haven't been intentional about fitting that activity into my daily (or honestly, yearly) schedule.

And every time we organize our house and Franklin sees the patterns and the machine, I get mocked for "*having to have,"* that sewing machine, *"for all the sewing"* I was going to do. Despite the fact that he's half kidding, his words still get under my skin and make me feel stupid and ashamed of my lofty ambitions.

Anyone relate? Ever get really jazzed up about an idea, a new workout program or new organization system and then after the buzz wears off you realize you don't have the energy, knowledge, or desire to sustain it? Good "ideas" don't lead to life change.

Inspiring vision + action steps = transformation.

We don't want this book to be another good theory. Everything we've talked about is possible to execute, maybe just not at once. If you try to succeed at them all, chances are you'll find yourself overwhelmed and frustrated at your perceived failure.

I (Sarah) started learning the guitar when I lived in France for a short time after high school. Some friends taught me casually as we were hanging out. I was so excited to take my newly acquired guitar knowledge back to the States with me after my stint in France was over. I loved to sing and had visions of being the next Dolores O'Riordon from The Cranberries (I know I just dated myself, go ahead and Google her). There is something so beautifully cathartic and powerful about playing an instrument while belting out tunes to a sold out coliseum...or so I could imagine.

I returned home and I found that guitars were expensive for a poor college student. Learning barre chords were hard! Getting callouses on my fingers was actually really painful. And just like that, my commitment to being the next guitar playing female rock star fell to the wayside. Since that I moment, I have often thought about the fact that had I stuck with the guitar, I would have been playing it for over 20 years by now. No, I probably wouldn't be experiencing life on the road as a talented performer, but I would have experienced decades of joy through playing while also developing a valuable skillset. This occurred to me as we were writing this book and it compelled me to pick up the guitar again. 'Cause even after 20 years, it's never too late to start again.

So we say, start now. Or start again. Pick 1 area from the book where you felt super inspired and start there. Let that be your reference point and don't work on anything else. Then choose an attainable action step. Maybe it's focusing on not talking about your body in a negative way or choosing to not argue with your partner when they say you're beautiful.

Choose something that feels attainable for you to do. As you start piling up little successes, you'll find yourself with the motivation and drive to tackle bigger areas of life change. Your numerous, smaller steps will prepare you to persevere in the really difficult changes. You'll also see the goodness waiting on the other side of the hard work and believe more deeply in the positive impact you're making.

Celebrate

The truth about change is, it's possible, it's a process, and it's worth it. Wall Street investor turned pastry chef Umber Ahmad says, [xxxv] *"There comes a point when you find the fire to do it for yourself. Balance isn't about giving enough energy to every single part of your life everyday. Balance is finding an inner peace knowing you are creating a legacy that will have an impact. You find the ability to give all you have and then forgive yourself for the places you couldn't reach."*

We hope we've sparked a fire in your heart that ignites your journey towards finding peace with your body. Yet even with this hope, our experience tells us there will still be certain days when your "fire" is hard to find and contentment feels a thousand miles away. This reality requires one last piece of our change puzzle: celebration.

As we choose to grow and move closer towards our reference point, we must remember that any forward movement, no matter the size, carries tremendous importance. As we make these decisions towards contentment, we pick up momentum. This momentum, over time, creates transformation. **It's not the end result we recognize. It's all the little choices we make along the way that deserve our celebration**. (Remember that growth mindset we're teaching our kids? Yeah, it's important for us too.)

So let's throw down and celebrate! Let's throw off the shackles that keep us prisoners of "the big."

The big weight loss number, the right size of clothing, or the sexy transformation story. We live in a culture of abundance and nothing seems valuable unless it's big. We believe differently.

I (Jenny) sat down to dinner the other night with my family. My daughter Luci wanted to pray before we ate. She began her usual prayer of gratitude going down the list of things for which her young mind was thankful. After she listed everyone and everything in our family, she ended by thanking God for herself. She literally said, *"thank you for me."*

In that moment I was stunned. I would never think to be thankful for me, to be thankful for who I am, let alone my body.

But I can be. We can be.

Let's spend time recognizing our forward movement and being thankful for our growth. We know there's a lot to be proud of.

Rupi Kaur, poetess and author of *Milk and Honey*[xxxvi] writes this:

"I want to apologize to all the women
I have called pretty
before I have called them intelligent or brave
I am sorry I made it sound as though
something as simple as what you're born with
is the most you have to be proud of when your
spirit has crushed mountains

from now on I will say things like
you are resilient or you are extraordinary
not because I don't think you're pretty
but because you are so much more than that."

Yes! We say "yes" to all of it and exclaim, "*We are so*
much more than our stomachs, our breasts, our hips, or our stretch
marks. We are more than multi-taskers, breast feeders, and
birthers, and way more than our eyes, skin, and smile. We are
more!"

And so we celebrate YOU. You've done hard work and
we're so proud. We're positive—if we were together—
we'd be wiping tears from our eyes with hearts full of
perspective and appreciation. You, friend, are simply
amazing.

You're strong.
You're courageous.
You're capable.
You're talented.
You're clever.
You're beautiful (inside and out).

You're an amazing woman, partner, friend, and mother.
Let it soak in; breathe it into your head and heart, letting
that truth wash over you. You are so much more and this
"more" is worth applauding.

One Day

"At first people refuse to believe that a strange new thing can be done, then they begin to hope it can be done, then they see it can be done--then it is done and all the world wonders why it was not done centuries ago." -Frances Hodgson Burnett, *The Secret Garden*

As our book journey comes to an end, we hope one day this struggle we fight is nothing more than a moment recorded in the history books. In its place we envision women walking unified in motherhood. The line is long, longer than any human eye can see, and the power is palpable. Our heads are held high with the peace and confidence contentment brings. Vulnerability and empathy become our war cry. As we walk, our enemies fall, first self-doubt followed by fear. Comparison and judgment run the other way while "normal" falls and dies. It has finally been vanquished once and for all.

Let's stand together setting self-hatred and self-loathing aside—judgment and jealousy can join the heap too—and let's celebrate every part of ourselves. Let's be kind in the embrace of vulnerability, dropping the façade we have been straining to keep in place (it's been sucking the life out of us anyway). Let's use our energy to genuinely connect. Together, we can embrace the moments we've worked hard to purposely arrive at and feel proud that contentment was our direction and we made it there.

We are Freedom Fighters and "normal" doesn't stand a chance.

Recap

- ✓ Don't drown your butterfly. Sometimes we accidentally kill what we deeply want because we aren't patient with the process.
- ✓ Good intentions coupled with intentional living create life change.
- ✓ It takes a lot of hard work to learn new habits and unlearn old ones. They die so hard, stubborn buggers.
- ✓ Sometimes our growth looks like tacking across the lake in a sailboat. There's a lot of zigging and zagging.
- ✓ Don't worry though! Celebrate it all. Forward movement of any kind is reason to celebrate. And a great way to do this is to cultivate an attitude of gratitude.

Action Steps
Journal or Discuss

We have 2 closing challenges for you. We're hopeful both of these become consistent rhythms in your life.

- ✄ The first one is to create a Gratitude List. It could be a piece of paper posted on the fridge that everyone in the family contributes to or it could be a pad of post-it notes you keep on your desk. The key is to keep an on-going list of the things you're grateful for (and something as simple as clean, folded laundry is totally legit.)

✖ The second challenge is to connect with a person and invite them to walk this contentment journey with you. It might feel a little like asking someone on a date, but trust us, life change is worth the risk. You might want to ask them to be an accountability partner with you. It could be helpful to read this book together to be on the same page (literally). But if not, catch them up to speed on what you're learning.

If you're up for it, ask to chat with them on a regular basis to help keep you engaged in the fight towards contentment. The ultimate goal here is growth through change. What that exactly looks like for you will be unique but if you'd like some direction—take a look at the action steps from each of the previous chapters.

Identify areas where you are strong and areas where you would like to grow.

As you connect through conversation, tackle one of the topics/sub-topics in each of the chapters.

Thank you.

Thank you for trusting us, but ultimately trusting yourself to travel down this treacherous road towards contentment. We believe in you. Keep fighting the good fight, mama. You're doing a great job.

If you would like to continue with us on this journey outside the pages of this book, we would love to have you virtually connect with us on our private Facebook group, The War On Normal. You can search for it under "Groups." It's an opportunity to use the medium of social media to foster real, life connections with women who live near you, because we believe we are stronger together.

If you'd like more information on the book, Jenny and Sarah or our speaking engagements, check out http://www.thewaronnormal.com

My Notes

JENNY BAKER & SARAH BLIGHT

End Notes

i http://www.surgery.org/media/statistics

ii http://www.huffingtonpost.com/2013/10/24/women-body-image_n_4156825.html

iii The Bible. (NIV). Phillippians 4:10-13

iv http://www.slate.com/articles/double_x/doublex/2011/04/why_wont_this_new_mom_wash_her_hair.html

v http://en.wikipedia.org/wiki/Kraamzorg

vi http://sjinsights.net/2014/09/29/new-research-sheds-light-on-daily-ad-exposures/

vii http://www.babycenter.com/0_the-new-mom-body-survey-7-000-women-tell-it-like-it-is_3653252.bc?showAll=true

viii http://www.redcrowmarketing.com/2015/09/10/many-ads-see-one-day/

ix https://www.psychologytoday.com/blog/communication-success/201510/14-signs-psychological-and-emotional-manipulation

x The Bible. (NIV) Ecclesiastes 1:9

xi http://www.cdc.gov/nchs/data/databriefs/db76.pdf

xii https://www.adaa.org/about-adaa/press-room/facts-statistics

xiii http://webstersdictionary1828.com/

xiv http://www.accademia.org/explore-museum/artworks/michelangelos-david/

xv http://edition.cnn.com/2008/WORLD/africa/06/24/mandela.quotes/

xvi https://www.washingtonpost.com/news/to-your-health/wp/2015/08/11/the-most-depressing-statistic-imaginable-about-being-a-new-

xvii http://psycnet.apa.org/?&fa=main.doiLanding&doi=10.1037/a0013969

xviii The Bible. (NIV) Philippians 4:8.

xix http://ww2.kqed.org/mindshift/2013/04/24/giving-good-praise-to-girls-what-messages-stick/

xx http://www.huffingtonpost.com/salman-khan/the-learning-myth-why-ill_b_5691681.html?1408465176

xxi http://www.dove.com/us/en/stories/about-dove/our-research.html

xxii http://www.usatoday.com/story/news/nation/2013/08/23/moms-daughters-influence-body-image/2690921/

xxiii The Bible. Proverbs 13:20

xxiv Janis, Irving L. (1982). Groupthink: Psychological Studies of Policy Decisions and Fiascoes. Second Edition. New York: Houghton Mifflin.

xxv http://www.huffingtonpost.com/andrea-bonior/carlin-flora_b_3388153.html

xxvi http://www.cloudtownsend.com/boundaries/

xxvii http://markmanson.net/boundaries

xxviii https://www.forbes.com/sites/bonniemarcus/2016/01/13/the-dark-side-of-female-rivalry-in-the-workplace-and-what-to-do-about-it/#5d401ab35255

[xxix] http://abcnews.go.com/Lifestyle/jealous-perfect-mom-friends/story?id=31800999

[xxx] The Bible. Proverbs 27:17

[xxxi] https://psychcentral.com/blog/archives/2009/05/12/8-ways-to-overcome-jealousy-and-envy/?all=1

[xxxii] Wendy Mass, Jeremy Fink and the Meaning of Life.

[xxxiii] The Bible. Romans 12:14-16

[xxxiv] https://www.mindtools.com/pages/article/newISS_96.htm

[xxxv] https://www.forbes.com/sites/jopiazza/2017/03/15/meet-the-woman-who-left-wall-street-to-open-a-bakery

[xxxvi] Rupi Kaur "Milk and Honey" http://amzn.to/1TJOXsV